WITH
TROUBLED

Children

AND
TEENAGERS

of related interest

**Helping Babies and Children Aged 0–6
to Heal After Family Violence**
A Practical Guide to Infant- and Child-Led Work
Dr Wendy Bunston
Foreword by Dr Julie Stone
ISBN 978 1 84905 644 1
eISBN 978 1 78450 138 9

The Simple Guide to Child Trauma
What It Is and How to Help
Betsy de Thierry
Foreword by David Shemmings
Illustrated by Emma Reeves
ISBN 978 1 78592 136 0
eISBN 978 1 78450 401 4

Healing Child Trauma Through Restorative Parenting
A Model for Supporting Children and Young People
Dr Chris Robinson and Terry Philpot
ISBN 978 1 84905 699 1
eISBN 978 1 78450 215 7

Supporting Traumatized Children and Teenagers
A Guide to Providing Understanding and Help
Atle Dyregrov
ISBN 978 1 84905 034 0
eISBN 978 0 85700 391 1

**A Practical Guide to Caring for Children and
Teenagers with Attachment Difficulties**
Chris Taylor
ISBN 978 1 84905 081 4
eISBN 978 0 85700 367 6

Working
WITH
TROUBLED
Children
AND
TEENAGERS

JONNY
MATTHEW

Jessica Kingsley *Publishers*
London and Philadelphia

First published in 2018
by Jessica Kingsley Publishers
73 Collier Street
London N1 9BE, UK
and
400 Market Street, Suite 400
Philadelphia, PA 19106, USA

www.jkp.com

Library of Congress Cataloging in Publication Data
A CIP catalog record for this book is available from the Library of Congress

British Library Cataloguing in Publication Data
A CIP catalogue record for this book is available from the British Library

ISBN 978 1 78592 393 7
eISBN 978 1 78450 752 7

Printed and bound in Great Britain

MIX
Paper from
responsible sources
FSC
www.fsc.org
FSC® C013056

For my lovely Karen.
Your dedicated hard work, gentle intelligence
and quiet professionalism
has changed the lives of many troubled children forever.
And mine.
You are an inspiration!

"Soli Deo Gloria."

Contents

Welcome

Our children are the rock on which our future will be built, our greatest asset as a nation.

Nelson Mandela

Thanks!

First of all, thanks for buying this book!

Why this book?

This little book is intended to be a helpful book, but it's also a kind of manifesto. It's a gathering together of positive beliefs and values for working with troubled young people.

There are a number of reasons why I wanted to write it:

- **To inspire.** Working with troubled young people – whatever their specific challenges – is demanding. If I can add some inspiration to help like-minded people to keep going, reflect and improve on what they do, all the better. Sometimes all it takes is a shot of encouragement or an inspirational thought and we're back on track.

- **To inform.** We all learn as we go along. We pick up little 'tricks of the trade'. We establish what works for us. I want to pass on some of what I've learned in 30+ years of working with young people. I hope it will help you crystallise your own ideas and maybe inspire some new ones.

Meet the author

Whenever I read something, I find it helpful to know a little about the author. I reckon I owe it to you to do the same for *my* readers, so here goes.

My passion is working to help young people in crisis to recover. I also like to inspire colleagues to do the same.

I left school at 16 to apprentice as a motor mechanic. I volunteered in a church youth club at the same time (I was the kid who wouldn't leave!). Later I qualified in social work, specialising in youth justice, before taking a Masters degree in criminology and criminal justice.

I have previously been a youth justice social worker for a local authority in a youth offending team and, for nearly ten years, a manager and specialist practitioner with Barnardo's Cymru Taith Service, working with children and young people with sexualised histories who are now displaying harmful sexual behaviour of their own.

One of my most challenging professional roles was being part of the management team at a Secure Children's Home. My responsibilities included interventions, care planning and staff training. Essentially, it was my job to lead the organisation in our endeavours to treat the problems of some of the country's most difficult and damaged children.

I currently work part-time as Practice Change Lead with the Youth Justice Board, in Wales. I'm helping to test a child development approach to complex and prolific offending young people.

My interests have broadened over the years to include anything relating to children and young people who, because of their experiences, have a troubled life and need help. Over the years, as my career has unfolded, I've found myself doing less direct work with children and a lot more helping those who do the helping.

This book is part of that: I want it to promote the rights, well-being and future success of young people whose start in life has been a struggle.

Maybe they've been abused, neglected, brain-injured or abandoned to the care system, or maybe they have a mental illness. Whatever the cause, life for many young people is tough. Very tough.

Finding a positive path

Many of us will be able to look back at decisions we've made which have led us down particular paths in life. I was one of those kids who could have gone either way: into trouble or on to success.

I found myself faced with two paths whilst sat in the back of a police car in 1982. Let's say I'd put a little more than a foot wrong, and the officer in question wasn't happy at all with me. It was a make or break moment. I was told I could either apologise, or be taken home in a police car and see him again in court.

As it happened, I was able to make the right decision. I made my apologies, ate a massive slice of humble pie, and the police officer let me go.

Looking back now I wonder how I kept my cool.

But, when I really think about it, the reason I was able to apologise becomes clear – it was because I'd had a great start in life, with dedicated, hard-working, loving parents who provided a moral framework for me to follow. I had a sense of how to respond to authority, and they taught me how to understand, control and deal with my emotions so I could make a rational decision under pressure.

In short, they gave me a road map to a good life – if I chose to follow it.

But many young people never experience that care. Their early years are characterised by threat, illness, neglect, abuse or a combination of these and more. They have no 'template' for decent behaviour. They don't regulate their emotions well. They live anxiously. And they make bad decisions or stumble into trouble because they have no road map to help them avoid it.

These kids deserve chances. It's our responsibility, wherever possible, to play a part in giving them those chances. And they deserve as many chances as they need in order to turn their lives around.

The importance of key adults

For most children, their best chance lies in building a trusting relationship with an adult who cares. Someone who can be their security and look out for their interests. Someone who knows the way and can guide them along. Someone who believes in them and doesn't give up when the road gets rocky or the young person veers off. And – perhaps most importantly of all – someone who doesn't give up, even when the young person gives up or does all they can to push people away. Someone – *anyone* – who gives a monkeys about them. These kids need someone like that.

Someone like you?

For many kids, that person is a professional. They might be a support worker or mentor, social worker, a foster or kinship carer, a therapist, a youth offending team worker, a youth worker, someone in residential childcare, or a school teacher.

It's less about the role or the title – it's all about *the person*.

Introduction

Reprimand not a child immediately on the offence. Wait till the irritation has been replaced by serenity.

Moses Hasid

When you encounter difficulties and contradictions, do not try to break them, but bend them with gentleness and time.

St Francis de Sales

Best insult ever!

The best insult I ever had from a young person was very graphic: 'F*** off you short-a***d Yorkshire c***.' It was brilliant!

Brilliant because it focussed on all the things he thought would hurt me: my size (not very tall!), my accent, and his thoughts about me. It was only a few words long. And it was cutting!

Reading this you may experience one of two responses to it:

1. **A chuckle to yourself**, as you recall similar experiences you've had, or

2. **Your defences kick in**, and you begin to feel a little angry or agitated about the fact that kids sometimes behave in this way.

This book is for people who are 'number 1s'.

'Number 2s' – are you willing to give this book a chance to change your thinking? Are you open to radically changing your practice, and engaging troubled young people in ways that will help them? If so, please carry on!

Helping troubled kids:
finger-waggers need not apply

You see, people who are 'number 2s' have a tendency towards a belief system typified by the following markers:

- Feeling offended by the things young people say to them, particularly personal insults.

- Seeing compliance to 'adult norms' as the main sign of a young person's progress.

- Focussing on behaviour rather than personality, obedience rather than character, likeability *now*, as opposed to potential for later development.

- Responding to the *behaviour* rather than the *person*.

- Focussing on how the conduct affects *them*, the adult; not what it says about the young person's current state of mind or their past experiences.

In short, these folk see their role as mainly being to 'patrol the boundaries' of what they consider to be 'good' behaviour and enforce them: enforcement being the main point.

Such people often find themselves in conflict with the children they work with and are, more often than not, the people on the receiving end of aggression and conflict.

Having said that, *anyone* working with troubled young people will end up dealing with aggression and offensive language at some point – it comes with the territory.

How we deal with difficult behaviour says a lot about how we understand young people in the first place.

Insults: what's going on?

Here's a quick summary of what's going on when young people start throwing out insults:

- **Communication** – the young person is making contact with us. This is a good thing, regardless of the content!

- **Information** – they are focussed on us and they are letting us know something about themselves, whether they mean to or not.

- **Emotion** – they're letting us know that there are strong feelings going on that have caused a particularly spirited response.

All this helps us. It might not *feel* helpful when we're in the moment. But it helps.

It helps us because it informs our understanding of the young person in front of us. It also equips us to help them to deal with the situation better: to get over the emotion of it, learn from it and move on.

My brain hurts!

Aggression from troubled kids isn't personal. Well, usually anyway…

Their aggression is rooted in the responses which have kept them safe and/or enabled them to cope whilst living in difficult and traumatic situations. Thinking of it as a reflex reaction, rather than a decision, can be a useful way to put it into perspective.

Children raised in trauma, fear or threat struggle to recognise, understand and contain their feelings. The more logical, thoughtful and reflective functions of the rational brain are overridden by the emotional surges and lack of control that years of problems have caused.

Understanding that we can't reason young people out of strong feelings, or command them into obedience through finger-wagging, is a great first step towards resolving aggressive outbursts.

When logic and reason are overwhelmed by tension and emotion, something has to blow. And it has to blow out fully before talking can really help.

Onward and upward

In this book I will lay out the kinds of values, attitudes and approaches which, in my experience, encourage effective engagement with troubled children and young people.

This is a journey that requires us to be open and willing to learn. Unless we are prepared to reflect on what we do, ask ourselves why we do it *that* way and how we can improve, we will short-circuit any hope of getting better at what we do and we'll never practise as effectively as we otherwise might!

We all have a little of the finger-wagger in us. But if that's your method, and you like it, put this book down now.

For those who recognise this tendency but want to do better – read on!

Postscript

Let me encourage you to wreck this book!

To get the most out of it, you should probably mark it, underline stuff, write in the margin, highlight bits, cross it out, even. But please don't read it passively.

I love it when I get to the end of a book and can look back over what I reacted to while reading it. I hope you'll do the same.

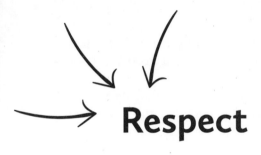

Chapter 1

Respect

> For to be free is not merely to cast off one's chains, but to live in a way that respects and enhances the freedoms of others.
>
> *Nelson Mandela*

> He removes the greatest ornament of friendship, who takes away from it respect.
>
> *Cicero*

When someone respects us, we know it. Somehow we can just tell. It's not necessarily the words they use. It's just apparent.

In fact, sometimes the words or actions someone uses might not be the ones we want to hear or see, but the respect comes through anyway. Respect is clear like that – you just know if it's there or not.

The same goes for troubled kids – they *know* when someone respects them.

How do you see troubled kids?

The best way to understand this idea, I think, is to answer the following. What's the basic *sense* you have of these kids, as people? How do you *see* troubled children and young people?

The bestselling author on leadership Stephen R. Covey tells a story that brilliantly illustrates this point in his book *The 7 Habits of Highly Effective People*.[1]

He describes a peaceful subway ride one day. People are quietly travelling home, some are nodding off, others are reading their newspapers. Everyone is quiet and generally minding their own business.

All of a sudden the peace is disturbed...

> Suddenly a man and his children entered the subway car. The children were so loud and rambunctious that instantly the whole climate changed.
>
> The man sat down next to me and closed his eyes, apparently oblivious to the situation. The children were yelling back and forth, throwing things, even grabbing people's papers. It was very disturbing. And yet, the man sitting next to me did nothing.
>
> It was difficult not to feel irritated. I could not believe that he could be so insensitive as to let his children run wild like that and do nothing about it, taking no responsibility at all. It was easy to see that everyone else on the subway felt irritated too. So, finally, with what I felt was unusual patience and restraint, I turned to him and said, 'Sir, your children are really disturbing a lot of people. I wonder if you couldn't control them a little more?'
>
> The man lifted his gaze as if to come to a consciousness of the situation for the first time and said softly, 'Oh, you're right. I guess I should do something about it. We just came from the hospital where their mother died an hour ago. I don't know what to think, and I guess they don't know how to handle it either.' (p.38)

Wow! What a moment. All of a sudden the scene takes on a whole different meaning.

---

1   Covey, S.R. (2013) *The 7 Habits of Highly Effective People*. New York: Rosetta Books.

Seeing things differently

Covey goes on to say that the man's response caused a paradigm shift to take place whereby he was forced to change his whole perspective.

Now he *saw* things differently. He saw *everything* differently:

- the behaviour of the children

- the apparent insensitivity of the father

- the reasons why the father didn't act sooner to quieten his kids.

Everything changed when he really knew what was going on.

This is what I'm talking about when I asked earlier, 'How do you *see* troubled children and young people?'

Getting to the bottom of this question is key for those of us who work with them. It'll tell us everything we need to know about our values, our motivations and our expectations.

So what's your answer? How do *you* see troubled kids? It might help to play a quick game of word association:

Action point: What words or phrases come into your mind first when you think about the kids you work with or care for? Make a note of these.

Now, we'll all have slightly different things to say here. Each of us has our own priorities. Whatever our answers, they are the key drivers behind what we do. They betray our true motives and values.

Seeing changes everything

When we see things differently, according to Stephen Covey, three things happen:

1. we **think** differently
2. we **feel** differently
3. we **behave** differently.

Not only did Covey's view of the man on the train change, his thoughts, feelings and behaviour all changed too. How he *saw* the man affected everything else.

How you and I see troubled kids influences everything else we do with them, how we think about them and how we interact with them.

Fundamentally, unless there is a core driver of respect for the child, we will lack something in the way we *see* them. That lack will limit and tarnish everything we do.

Equally, and conversely, if there is a foundation of respect, it will shine through in the way we think, feel and behave towards them and their families.

If there is a foundation of respect it will shine through!

The ingredients of respect

So, how can we know whether or not we are seeing troubled kids respectfully, and in a way that drives and energises our work in a respectful way?

Here are a few points to think about:

- **Acceptance of value as a person.** Because problems are at the centre of the work we do, it's easy to forget the bigger picture. This is a *person* we are dealing with. Someone with their own thoughts and feelings. They have hopes and aspirations, just like us. But, unlike us, they lack power and influence. They don't have the education, physical strength or authority that we have. Because of this we can forget that they are people of value, just like us. Acceptance of this, and them, is crucial

 Respect conveys that we understand their equality of personhood; we value them as people.

- **Recognising blamelessness.** Similarly, our focus on problems means we can often forget how kids got to where they are today. They are people whose situation in life has brought them to where they are – almost certainly it's a place they wouldn't choose. But they didn't *have* a choice, did they? Maybe their parents did. Maybe the people who mistreated them had options. They made decisions. And those decisions meant this child or young person ended up where they are today. But the child is blameless.

 Respect will always take account of and allow for someone's victimisation experiences and its impact on their development.

- **Believing that people are equal.** Personhood is a fundamental state of *being*. By virtue of being people, we are all in some essential way entirely equal. We may possess unequal power compared to others. We may be unequal in our influence over people or events around us. But we do possess absolutely equal *value*, regardless of contribution, and no matter how pleasing or problematic this is. These children and teenagers are equal in value to us. Their life chances have been different. Their current situation certainly is. They may not contribute anything valuable to society just yet. But, underneath it all, they are exactly like us, and equal to us in value.

Respect conveys the degree to which we value someone.

- **Seeing your work as 'service'.** Our role is to serve. I'm not talking about our professional duties here. This is not about the minutiae of what we are expected to do, our daily tasks, etc. This is about the way we see ourselves in relation to the child. We are here to *serve* them. First and foremost. Not ourselves, our agency or even our mortgage. But *them*. We are here *for* them. To help *them*. When we reduce our roles to fulfilling certain agency duties, we miss the point. The child or young person *is* the point. Our true role is to serve them and their best interests.

If we truly respect a young person, then it can naturally lead to an attitude of service.

None of us can realistically expect to operate on these terms all the time. None of us is 100 per cent consistent in the way we function. We get tired, we have a frazzled start to the day, and things challenge us in our own lives.

But if there is an underlying respectfulness in the way we view the children we serve, it will come across. It will motivate and direct our attitudes and our actions *most* of that time.

And when we get it wrong and score an own goal, we can acknowledge it, learn from it, apologise, move on, and seek ways to avoid making the same mistake again.

 Respect is not about being super-human: just human. And treating others as such.

The power of respect

Fundamental to this notion of respect in professional practice is its relationship with power. A person who is disempowered by society at large and their own experiences can be empowered when shown true respect from professionals. There are two facets of empowerment going on here:

1. That which comes *implicitly* from being properly respected.

2. That generated from the efforts to *explicitly* and actively give power to people.

So, for example, if I treat someone with respect it elevates them from their usual sense of *not* being respected – *implicit* empowerment. If my role is to help them understand certain information, then I'm empowering them to make an informed decision – *explicit* empowerment.

True respect is the great equaliser. It flattens out the playing field. To paraphrase the quote from Nelson Mandela which opens this chapter, our freedom to exercise respect in our professional practice can enhance the freedom of others – in this case, the kids we serve.

If we really want to empower these children we should strive to imbue everything we do with respect.

Doing so can lift troubled children and young people to a new level. It starts with a feeling. A feeling they get from us and the way we treat them. How we speak. Our demeanour. The focus we have on listening to them. Our serving attitude.

Importantly, this feeling can evolve beyond a feeling generated by someone *else*. Once you feel respected, you can start to respect *yourself*. Respect from others is the foundation of *self*-respect.

If we truly respect children, they can begin to learn to respect themselves.

Self-respect as an engine of real change

Most of the children and young people in the care and criminal justice systems, in mental health units and secure children's homes, in prisons and pupil referral units, and in foster or kinship care have had a really poor roll of the dice. An underlying reason behind the developmental impairment of many troubled children and young people is the failure of caregivers to love and care for them properly.

The result of such failing is a child who hasn't learned their own value: they don't respect themselves because they can't.

But they can begin to learn how from caring adults.

As you move through the chapters in this book keep in mind this central principle:

 The way I see a child or young person will influence everything I do.

This can be:

- my thoughts and ideas
- my speech and behaviour
- the decisions I make.

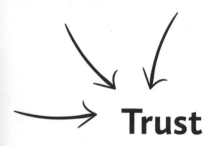

Chapter 2

Trust

Without trust, words become the hollow sound of a wooden gong. With trust, words become life itself.

John Harold

I think that John Harold had it about right. Without trust words mean nothing.

The kids we work with have larned this well – through bitter experience. They have learned to survive against the odds. They are the 'Artful Dodgers' of today. They know about *not* trusting people.

What is trust?

Let's start by looking at what trust actually is. What does it mean?

- Relying on the integrity, strength or ability of a person or thing.

- Being confident in expecting something.

- A person you rely on.

So trust is a pretty big thing.

It has to do with a real belief in someone and their reliability – a belief that they are someone we can lean on. Someone we expect to do what they say they'll do; someone who'll deliver.

This is what troubled kids need – someone who can be this for them.

Qualifications aren't enough

A friend of mine, Andy, is in his late fifties and has just retired after suffering a major health setback. He's had a long career as a schoolteacher and then as a civil servant. He worked hard to support and develop systems and people who deal with troubled teenagers, and now the time's come to kick back and enjoy himself.

Between his savings, the sale of his parents' house and the lump sum from his early retirement, he has a hefty pile of money to keep him going.

But there's a problem. He has no idea how to invest it. He needs help. But who do you ask for help with investing your nest egg?

Someone you trust, right? Of course! No one would give their dosh to someone who is less than completely trustworthy.

So I introduced Andy to my brother, who is a chartered financial planner. Pete knows what he's doing with money. But that wasn't enough for Andy.

Being my brother wasn't enough either. Being one of the most highly qualified advisers in the country wasn't enough. Writing an award-winning blog and podcast about personal financial management wasn't enough. Managing a whole team of financial consultants and looking after millions of pounds of other people's money wasn't enough.

Only *trust* would do.

So I introduced them and they met. They talked. And then they met and talked again. And again. And again.

They got to know each other. Pete found out what Andy wanted. Then he made a plan and they discussed it, changed it and discussed it some more.

Eventually, several months later, Andy handed over *some* of his dosh to Pete for investment. Not all of it. *Some* of it.

Sequencing matters

You see, Andy needed to trust Pete *before* he parted with his cash. The sequence really matters. Trust first. Cash second.

Children and young people who struggle to trust need time. They won't fully engage with us until they trust us. There's no shortcut. Trust first. Engagement second.

Here are some of the reasons why the children we work with find trusting others difficult:

- **Because people have let them down** – family, friends, professionals, services, society in general. Often these children have *tried* to trust others but have been let down. Things haven't worked out as planned. So they are slow to trust again. Understandably, they ask questions like, 'Why should I trust *you*? What makes *you* different?'

- **Because trust is hard to do** – not least because it hasn't worked out before. But also, when you've had horrible experiences, you learn that the only way to be sure is to trust your*self*. At least then when things go wrong, there's no one else to blame. Laying yourself open to being let down, again, is a tough call for anyone – particularly a child.

- **Because 'I've done OK so far'** – OK, so things aren't perfect. By a long way! But I'm still here. I'm still trying. As measures of success go in a challenging life, that's not a bad outcome. So why would I risk shortening the odds by trusting someone else? Anyway, I don't know anyone *that* reliable. And I have no way of knowing if *you'll* be reliable either.

- **Because as time goes on it gets harder** – we all rely on ourselves as much as possible. But most of us have others we can lean on when things get tough. Young people have often gone a very long time without having someone they can rely on. That makes trusting a massive challenge.

With all of these reasons to be sceptical about trusting people, it's really important that we get the sequencing right for the kids we work with.

 Trust comes first, then engagement. It has to be in that order!

It's tough on our own

Our instinct as human beings is to trust others.

Part of us wants to trust because it's intrinsic to our nature. That's why there's hope for us with these young people – because something inside of them *wants* to let go and trust someone.

It's hard to do it all by yourself. One might even say we are designed as social beings – we're not fully ourselves unless we have some degree of inter-dependence with others.

We all suffer various challenges during our lives. Money worries, illness, losses, relationship struggles. But there is a unique pain to feeling isolated.

Being disconnected or *un*connected places us in a position that other struggles do not. We are alone. We can be left feeling that, despite being *in* the world, we are somehow not *part* of it.

This has a sting all of its own.

Unique pain

I'll never forget one young man I worked with who taught me this lesson loud and clear.

We'd been working together – supposedly addressing his offending – for over a year. But I'd spent nearly all of that time building trust and establishing a relationship. A bond through which he might find a way to be able to trust me.

Over the preceding few weeks he'd started to trust me and had talked a lot about his early life. About the multiple abuses he'd suffered. About the neglectful parenting from his Mum, who was struggling to keep her own body and soul together, let alone those of her young son.

He talked about poverty, about violence in the home, about a lack of food and about the strangers constantly calling at the house.

He had vivid memories of feeling frightened that his mother would die and leave him forever. He gave a graphic account of the two occasions he'd found his mother in the throes of attempting suicide and how he called the paramedics who had managed to save her just in time.

During one session I asked this young man what the most poignant recollection was. Which of his memories was the thing that stuck in his mind the most. I expected him to pick out one of the long list of things we'd talked about. But he didn't.

After a brief, thoughtful pause, he said something completely new that he hadn't mentioned before. Here's what he said: 'I was lonely, Jonny.'

The power of neglect

Of all the abuses, neglect is the one that undermines development the most.

Bad parenting is one thing. Abusive treatment is another. But, with neglected children, the almost complete lack of parenting brings a uniquely isolating and distancing impact on the growing child.

- **Neglect is isolating.** When children are not responded to in a sensitive and nurturing way, they suffer problems. But when a parent just doesn't respond at all, or rarely, then the child is left alone to try to make sense of their bodies, their feelings, their environment, their lives. Without language, without meaning and without resolution, the infant child's subjective state is one of implicit and overwhelming aloneness. Isolated. They are separate and unknowing.

- **Neglect is numbing.** Responsive parents help their children to understand themselves through providing care. Our soothing and calming efforts give meaning to the child's experiences. Without this meaning-making, children are left bereft, without meaning, without understanding and without relationship. Without definition or knowledge about their own experiences, they are anaesthetised to what's going on in and around them. Without the reflective sounding board of an attentive parent, they are numb.

- **Neglect is distancing.** The uniquely interpersonal nature of the parent–infant bond is key to normal development. Without it, children not only become numb to themselves, they become numb to others. Neglected children miss that essential early learning that others matter, that they are dependent on those around them to some degree. Instead, they live life at a distance from other people. As if on an island of isolated experiences. Separate and disconnected.

Neglected children miss out on one of the key lessons of early life: big people (adults) are trustworthy; they respond and they help. It's difficult for us to imagine how impossibly hard it must be for such children to begin to trust other people. Particularly others with whom they have no meaningful connection – like professionals. Add to this the obvious fact that we are involved because there are problems of some kind that require our input. We are there because something went wrong!

Why would they trust us? What reason do they have to even *believe* that others are worthy of their trust? Let alone worthy of the gargantuan effort it's going to take to try to actually get to the point where they feel that they *can* trust.

Earn it: first, by hanging in there

Given all this, we shouldn't be surprised that we have to *earn* the trust of troubled children and young people.

We don't deserve it. It's not our right. We have to do the hard graft of being worthy, of being safe and of hanging in there long enough to merit the accolade 'trustworthy'.

Infants have no choice but to learn from their parent. Teenagers are different. They can choose whether to trust *people* or not. They can vote with their feet any time they like. And they do. Who can blame them?

So one of the ways we can begin to earn trust is to accept young people *as they are.*

This is really about one simple message – that they don't have to earn *our* involvement, we have to earn theirs!

Earning trust

I was over a year into working with a 15-year-old young man. We were addressing his offending – serious offending. For a number of months I'd been encouraging him to talk about his background. Particularly some of the dreadful things I knew must have happened to him – though he'd never told a soul about them.

One day he entered the room for a session and something was different. Gone was the friendly bravado, the mickey-taking and the banter. Today something was different.

There was no greeting, no asking how I was, no easy exchange of witticisms. He just pointed at my pen and paper, and said, 'I'll speak. You write.'

And for almost two hours he relayed how he'd been serially abused by four different men – all partners of his mother – violently, emotionally, sexually.

It took him over a year of working every week to feel ready to talk. More than that, it took a year for him to be able to *trust enough* to talk. To earn trust, we have to hang in there.

If we can earn their trust, I believe there are a number of key outcomes for the children and young people we serve. These include:

- **They'll listen.** Troubled young people have learned to survive. Often they do this through a process of realisation that others cannot be trusted. They let you down. They disappoint. They hurt and abuse. They reject and abandon. When young people meet someone whose care and concern connects with them, they notice the difference. Once this occurs, they are more inclined to listen and to take on board what's being said. Win their trust and young people will usually give you a fair hearing, even when you have to say unpalatable things.

- **They'll speak.** One of the great challenges is being able to tap into the real thoughts and opinions of the young people themselves. Too often decisions are made based on what we *think* is in their best interests. Wouldn't it be great if we could really *know*? If young people trust us, they are more likely to be honest with us. This is, perhaps, the greatest compliment of all.

- **They'll be influenced.** Damaged and difficult young people are no different from the rest of us. They are influenced by people they are impressed with or have some affinity for. Trustworthy people who care are among the most influential. Would you undergo an operation from a surgeon you knew but didn't trust? Neither would I. So why would a young person allow someone to influence them if they didn't know, like or trust them? Exactly.

- **They'll initiate.** Some young people get assessed half to death. Despite our concerted efforts to find out what young people want, it remains a challenge to know what *they* think. How much better would it be if we could just ask them and get a straight answer? Trust oils the wheels of honesty. It allows us to say things which might otherwise put us in a vulnerable position, leaving us exposed. But if we have faith in the person we're talking to, we feel safer, and more able to share openly. Young people are no different. When they can rely on us, *they'll* start to take the initiative and ask for help. Then we're really rocking and rolling!

- **They'll soften.** Much of our initial contact with young people falls well short of meeting 'the real' person. We all wear masks; we give a different impression in different settings, depending on whom we're with or what our role is. Young people do this too. It takes a while to get through to the real person underneath. But once they begin to trust us, the mask will slip and the child's true self will feel safe enough to interact with us. That's when the progress really starts.

- **They'll mature** – eventually! The march of time and the added maturity this brings is a huge factor influencing desistance from crime, for example. Possibly the *biggest* factor. Many other problematic behaviours in children also fade with age. A trusting dyad – a two-person partnership – is a sure way of facilitating this process such that the influence of earlier difficulties is diluted. When this happens it allows the young person to move on. It's as if being anchored with someone who is secure, consistent and trustworthy allows them to relax and grow up.

If you think about it, this is an amazing return on our investment. We care; young people change.

OK, so it's a bit more tricky and involved than that! And it takes a while, sometimes years.

But for those of us who get out of bed because we can't help ourselves but care for these kids, it's great to know that we're on the right track and that our commitment to them and to the work is what fuels the best chances of change.

Comply or else

Adults often give children the message that if they don't comply, then… Well, you can fill in the rest for yourself. But essentially this is saying that we require them to do, to be or to say something particular, if we are going to work together.

- **In youth justice.** Young people have to comply with the conditions of the Court order or they'll breach them.

- **In foster care or a children's home.** Young people need to behave in a certain way or they have to move on (despite the monumental patience of carers).

- **In school.** Young people have to show respect, conform to classroom rules and work quietly or they'll be marked down or, in the worst cases, excluded.

- **On the street.** Young people can't congregate in groups or play around and shout too much or they'll get a Criminal Behaviour Order (or CRIMBO for short) – the replacement for what used to be called ASBOs.

- **In exams.** Young people must regurgitate facts in a way we deem to be both appropriate and correct, or they 'fail'.

- **In public.** Young people must dress in a way that doesn't offend or we'll look down on them and treat them prejudicially.

And on it goes.

Now, I'm being provocative here, but I'm doing it to highlight a real point – that we have structured how we operate as a society in a way that makes it hard – if not impossible – for troubled kids to trust us and feel a part of society *with* us.

We don't start with where *they* are at. We start with requiring them to come over here, to where *we* are. They have to be like us, or else.

Wrong message

If you think about it, this approach gives a very damning message. Not just that they have to be like us. What this really communicates is: *what you are* isn't good enough.

Have you ever turned up at a party or event and felt under-dressed? You feel like the poor relation! You know that people will be making assumptions about you based purely on your appearance. And this is so *not* what you're really like!

It feels unjust, unfair, inaccurate and downright frustrating. That's what kids feel like when we judge them. Only more so.

An example from my own practice demonstrates this:

> *I approached a little boy in the court waiting area to see if he was OK. He looked about ten years old, was sitting alone and seemed very small amongst all the adults and professionals milling around. But this was a criminal court, he was due to appear, and my job – as court officer that day – was to ensure he was safe and understood what was going on. So I said, 'Hi, my name's Jonny. If you need any help, just let me know.'*
>
> *He looked at me with utter disdain, swung his legs down off the seat, reached into his back pocket and produced a knife. As he pushed the blade out with his*

thumb, he said, 'I've been looking after myself for years, thanks. If I need anything, I'll sort it out myself.'

Oh dear! He was actually 14 years old and something of an old hand at dealing with pretty much anything a court could throw at him. I'd jumped to the conclusion that his size meant he was young and might need me.

My well-meaning but clumsy effort to help had told him that I thought he was vulnerable and likely to need me. Trust took a while to establish, and all the more so because he knew I neither knew him nor understood his situation – I had judged him on the basis of what I saw.

We worked together for the next couple of years and got on well, eventually. But things may have started better had I not judged him wrongly in the first place.

Sequencing again

So, if we are to ever help these children overcome their difficulties and make a good go of their lives, we have to meet them where they are *now*. It's all about sequencing, and in this order:

1. acceptance
2. trust
3. engagement
4. change.

If young people can feel that we aren't judging them but, on the contrary, that we accept them as they are, then there's a hope that they will feel safe enough to trust us.

If we can afford kids the respect of acceptance, then we're on our way to real change. Demanding conformity doesn't work.

Acceptance and trust come first. Only then can we help them to change.

Chapter 3

Motivation

Ability is what you're capable of. Motivation determines what you do.

Lou Holtz

What got you out of bed this morning to work with or look after troubled children or young people?

I know it probably wasn't the money!

It certainly wouldn't be the hassle and aggravation that working with disturbed children or resistant teenagers and their families can bring. And I doubt the lack of resources, training and clinical supervision persuaded you either.

But something drove you to get up and go at it again for another day. So what was it?

It's worth spending a little time to think through exactly what your motivations are.

Establishing our 'why' and keeping it in clear view is a valuable safeguard against all sorts of stuff; things like:

- losing focus

- running out of steam

- falling into bad work habits.

Why do such challenging work?

Personally, I think reflection is a good thing. In all spheres of life, it pays to stop for a moment now and then, to take stock. To think through why it is that we do what we do. Otherwise the busyness of life and work can just carry us along. We can lose our sense of doing things deliberately and for a reason.

At best this ends up in a kind of malaise. Doing what we've always done. At worst, it allows us to develop bad habits, short-cuts, assumptions and default ways of doing things which go unchallenged.

The result of all this, of course, is that the best interests of the children we work with get diluted. Or lost altogether! At the very least they fade behind the need to fulfil the obligations of paperwork, accountability, policies and systems.

Cynicism sets in and the cycle continues.

How many colleagues have you met who exude a kind of resistant resignation to their role? I wonder how this impacts on the outcomes for the children and young people they work with.

Poor reasons for working with children and young people

There are many reasons for choosing to work with troubled kids. I don't think there is one definitive 'good' reason.

But, looking back on the people I've met over the years, I'm left with a clear sense that there *are* some *bad* reasons for a career in helping troubled children and teenagers.

Below are a few that come to mind.

To pay the mortgage

These are folk who do the job because 'it's a job'. They need to work to pay the mortgage. They may or may not actually *like* children, but they ended up working with them anyway. Maybe they started with a passion and it faded. Maybe they fell into it, without any sense of real deliberation. Maybe their own parents did it, so they followed – whether they wanted to or not. But the fact is that they just turn up, do their hours and go home again. There's no vision or real conviction in what they do. It's not a vocation. It's a job. Just a job.

I think of this as a kind of toxic passivity. It seems benign on the surface. But as you look at it closely, problems emerge. As we've discussed in the previous chapters, troubled young people are very astute; they may be socially inept or immature, offending or using drugs, but they *know* when someone 'gives a damn' within about 15 seconds of meeting them.

We all have bills to pay, clothes to get and food to buy; there's no shame in taking the money at the end of the month. Of course!

But if that's *all* it is. Or, sadly, if that's what it's *become*, maybe it's time to take stock and make some changes; or maybe it's too late and the time has come to do something else?

To meet personal needs

These are folk who struggle to separate their own difficulties from those of troubled young people. Whilst it can be argued that our own life experiences add empathic weight and insight to our work at times, it can be a real problem if we 'work out' our issues through helping others. Whether it's troubled self-esteem, misplaced feelings of guilt, anxiety around sexuality, parental rejection, depression, an identity issue, the need to feel we are useful or that we are a worthy person, or indeed any other challenging life situation. If it's our driver or motivation, it's a problem.

Principally, we can become blinkered and lose our objectivity. Being someone who cares and is objective, all at the same time, is hard enough as it is. Doing this when we are caught in the undertow of our own personal problems is nigh on impossible.

Everyone has issues and things to cope with in life. We all collect the odd scar along the way. But those who are professional helpers must first get help themselves. Only *then* can we help others effectively.

This is much like all good therapeutic training. Those being trained to provide therapy are required to go through the process of therapy themselves. They first have to experience the medicine they'll be dishing out to others. The development of self-reflection, and the insight that this brings, is invaluable in helping us to become better helpers.

Actually, I think it's crucial.

So if you have unresolved things to deal with, deal with them. Take time to look after yourself first (more on this later). Get help. Then you can use your own position of strength to focus fully on working for the good of others.

To salve their conscience

These folk are not at ease with themselves. They have a restless agitation about them. They carry the burden of the work too personally. That is, they believe that they have an obligation to effect change. They may be driven by anger, fear, guilt or quiet desperation. Whatever it is, it's about *them* and their need to fix things.

The problem here is that we are not dealing with widgets on a production line. We are dealing with people. Children – and damaged children at that.

The best of us can't be changed by the wilful efforts of others. We have to have sufficient *insight* and *desire* to change *ourselves*, albeit with the help of those around us. How much more is this the case for those with complex and deep-rooted challenges that go back years and have impacted on their development as people?

If we are to engage effectively with troubled young people, and if we are to work with colleagues and agencies to facilitate change, we must first be focussed on those who need us. And not be driven or preoccupied by our own needs.

Of course, no one fits any of these categories precisely. And we all have our weaknesses and failings. Arguably, none of us has entirely pure motives.

But there are plenty of professionals working with extremely demanding people whose effectiveness is hamstrung by one or a combination of these traits.

The best reason for working with children and young people

So, if it's not OK to do this work merely to pay the mortgage, to meet our own needs or to salve our conscience, what are the *right* reasons? There's only one in my book: care.

You have to care. You have to give a monkeys what happens to children and teenagers. The implications for this are huge.

 Whether or not young people believe that we care will affect pretty much everything we do with or for them.

In my experience, this belief will stem from a judgment about whether or not they can trust us. And it's a lot easier to trust someone who cares.

We talked about trust in the previous chapter, but it's worth adding that trust is the great multiplier. Trust can accelerate progress. Trust can help to encourage, motivate and cajole a reluctant person to change – but it will only be established if we genuinely care!

Chapter 4

Expectations

I believe that everyone is the keeper of a dream – and by tuning into one another's secret hopes, we can become better friends, better partners, better parents...

Oprah Winfrey

Think back to your own childhood and how you were parented.

Do you recall being constantly criticised? Did your parents/carers leave you completely to your own devices, boundariless and unguided? Did you feel your life or health was in danger because of the people you lived with?

In most people's experiences, including mine, the answer is 'No'.

I can vividly remember occasions, outside the home, where I felt unsafe, as you might have felt too. Home was the place to go when things go wrong or you need some sense of safety and reassurance – a safe harbour in the storm.

Such associations with 'home' are simply not there for some children.

When home is a difficult or a dangerous place to be, it ceases to be a place you *want* to be. It's not a place you want to replicate. You don't grow up thinking, 'I want my home to be like that.'

Laying the groundwork

Most of us have standards and expectations for our lives and those around us because we were given these standards by our parents They taught them to us. They helped us to learn them. They exemplified them.

People we loved, trusted and respected made it clear what was expected of us. They encouraged us to achieve, to have a go and to do our best.

Without this, a person's expectations, if they have any at all, are skewed. They lack a standard to attain to, a template to work with and any sense of what success might look and feel like.

Our role then, as those tasked with helping these children and young people who have not had the opportunity to learn from such standards and expectations, is to help them discover their potential.

 Help them form their own expectations about life. About their own abilities and the possibilities these afford.

Here are some ways to help:

- **Capacity.** A child needs to be helped to establish what they might be capable of. It's a natural response to want the best for the kids we work with or parent, but to do this we need to know about their abilities. This is not just a plea for realism, to avoid pressing a child to perform beyond their abilities. It's more than that:

    - **Range** – how *broad* are their abilities? Are they physically able? Do they have intellectual potential? What about confidence levels? Are they aspirational?

    - **Type** – what *sorts* of things do they show talent for? Artistic, organisational, thoughtful, practical, dramatic, physical, creative, risk-taking, musical, etc.

- **Interest.** Discover what level of interest the young person shows in different things. Most of us develop abilities or knowledge about the things we are most interested in. Helping young people identify their own preferences can be a real step forward.

This is why the establishment of trust, and with it clearer communication and honesty, is so important. To help a young person, we must know them. Time spent building the relationship, and the trust that comes with it, is a very sound investment.

In this context we can help them see that feeling good about doing certain kinds of things can be a useful guide. Not all work has to *feel* like work. It's OK for it to be fun too.

And if something is enjoyable we'll more easily stick at it. If it's interesting we'll more readily learn about it. If we discover the capacity and latent ability to succeed at something – even on a small scale – we'll be energised by the encouragement this brings.

Helping kids discover the capacities and interests they have is key in helping them to form their expectations as well as ours.

Aim high and speak 'up' to young people

Once you have a sense of capacity and interest, you can begin to encourage. This encouragement should not be airy-fairy 'you can do anything if you really try' sort of rubbish.

It needs to be measured, specific encouragement grounded in what the young person has the capacity and interest for. In this way, they can start achieving sooner. And there's nothing like early success to put a spring in your step, keep you focussed and spur you on for more!

Some other things we can do to speak 'up' to young people:

- **'When', not 'if'.** Sometimes 'if' is appropriate. For example, '*If* you decided to apply for college...' But often we can help to encourage young people towards progress by using the language of positive

47

assumption and aspiration. For example, '*When you're through this tricky period...*' This has the positive assumption of progress built in. This kind of prospective positivism is a way of punctuating our speech with good messages. It shows our confidence in the young person. It demonstrates that we think of them as capable of change. The real coup comes when they start to speak this way themselves!

- **'I like this about you.'** Troubled young people may go months or even years without hearing a compliment. Developmentally speaking, they've not had the praise that children need to develop in a balanced way. The way they view themselves and their understanding about how others see them is tarnished by a lack of affirmation. In the worst cases they may have had just the opposite – a lifetime of criticism, verbal abuse and emotional rejection. We can begin righting this wrong very quickly after we meet them. 'I heard things went well in your meeting the other day – well done.' 'Julie tells me you're ironing your own clothes – you're looking smart.' 'Thanks for washing up – it's a real help.' Little comments, that's all.

 Little comments that reinforce, affirm and highlight positive traits, abilities and behaviours are powerful.

One young man that I worked with for nearly two years taught me this. During a session he pulled his hoodie down over the top of his face and eyed me menacingly from under it. 'What do you think of me when I do this?' he asked. 'Does it scare you?'

Now this conversation could have gone a number of different ways. I could have tried to ignore it or move on quickly and re-focus him on the 'work' at hand. I could have relied on our mutual humour and used some form of banter to deflect it away.

Instead I cashed in on the chance to be positive. 'Well, if I didn't know you, I might be a bit intimidated,' I said. 'But I know you're a really nice lad and I enjoy working with you. So, no, it doesn't scare me at all.'

A simple encounter, used in a positive way to build him up. Either of the other options would have been OK – nothing wrong with them at all. But by using this approach, he was encouraged and I was able to build him up a little in a perfectly natural way. Easy, and yet such responses can make a profound difference.

More things we can do to speak 'up' to young people include:

- **Thanks.** Respect for someone is easily demonstrated by the way we speak and the way we value what they do. The common courtesy of saying 'thank you' is a simple example. It tells the young person that we've noticed what they did or said, that we value it and that we're willing to point it out. Anything that builds, encourages and reinforces in this way is both easy and influential. Children and young people often trust us with information about themselves, their families, their thoughts. This takes guts. We should thank them for trusting us.

  - 'That must have been hard to say. Thanks for trusting me with it.'

  - 'That was a good piece of work. Thanks for sticking with it.'

  - 'Thanks for today, I really enjoyed it.'

  - 'Thanks for coming in on time, I appreciate it.'

  - 'Thanks for helping me out with that, you made it a lot easier.'

We'd speak like this to our partner, our colleagues and our friends. So why not to the kids we're working with?

- **Sorry.** We all score own goals now and then. The best thing we can do when this happens is to admit it, apologise and move on. For example, let's say I double-book an appointment and decide I need to re-arrange to see a young person another time instead. I should start with an apology that acknowledges that this isn't really acceptable, that it inconveniences them and that I regret having to do it. I still do it, but I've communicated it in a respectful, honest and honouring way. If we mess up, we should put our hand up, plead guilty and apologise.

  - 'I'm sorry about today, I double-booked and can't make it. But I'll arrange to come again as soon as possible.'

  - 'I'm late. I should have set off earlier. I'm sorry.'

  - 'I forgot to remind you about... I should have remembered. I'm sorry.'

In essence, we should apply the same principles to our interactions with children and young people as we would with colleagues. Why do we sometimes feel it's OK not to extend them the same courtesies? It isn't.

Speaking 'up' to young people in this way demonstrates respect and empowers them through affirming their worth and through diminishing – appropriately – our own. It says that we're not so important as to be above apologising to a child or young person.

And, after all, we want them to develop into adults who treat others well and behave respectfully. What better way to teach this than by demonstrating it ourselves? Pro-social modelling sounds posh and complicated, but it's essentially about being the kind of person we want others to become.

Again, when we show respect like this, we will find it reciprocated. This builds trust. And trust is everything.

Expect the unexpected!

Every child is different. No charge for that pearl of wisdom! But it's an easy one to forget.

How often have you worked with (or parented) a young person only to be disappointed with how they behave? Or the results they get? Or the preferences they express, whether it's about sport, the boyfriend or girlfriend they choose, or about serious decisions they have to make?

Yes, me too.

Whilst this is normal, there is one ingredient that we all fall for at some point. We have a clear idea of what 'success' will look like. In our mind's eye, we know what we're hoping for, what we're expecting.

And *that's* the problem. It's what *we're* expecting, what *we're* hoping for.

This simple skewing of what I call the 'expectation agenda' sets up many professional and parental relationships to be governed by tension, disagreement and conflict. We want one thing, they want another.

Here are some ways in which we can try to avoid this pitfall:

- **Stay child-centred.** It's not about us – it's *their* potential we're working to realise. We should remind ourselves of this regularly. What is it that they want? What outcomes are they hoping for? How do they want their future to look – today, tomorrow, next year?

- **Become a success-spotter.** Improvement is anything better than what went before. Anything. Make it your business to look for these things and to point them out. This takes a bit of practice. Be deliberate in searching out positives. Listen not only to *what* they say but *how* they say it.

Becoming a success-spotter is really about looking at the young person through different eyes.

- **Seize opportunities to praise.** Include the unexpected. If we have a clear idea in *our* minds about what success will look like, we'll miss the successes that are right under our noses. The ones that weren't in our minds, but are nonetheless real and praiseworthy. This is the work of a skewed expectation agenda – sometimes we don't see the little successes and gains because they don't match what we want them to be achieving. When we spot a success, we should point it out and then offer praise – a simple 'well done' will do it.

- **Encourage, encourage, encourage.** Once you spot success, however small, bring it to the child's attention. Remind them of it later, especially during more challenging times. Shining a light on even the simplest thing, and using it to encourage, is gold dust! So easy to do and yet so profound in its cumulative impact over time. Waiting for big gains is a mistake. Spot the little ones and keep the encouragement flowing! Be proactive. Make it your mission to encourage.

Speaking 'up' to young people and focussing on them and their definitions of success will help us to form the right expectations about what we're working towards. What *they're* working towards.

It's the difference between working for compliance with *our* expectations and working to help the young person realise what it is *they* want.

A conflicted expectation agenda undermines our ability to work together with children to find and achieve their goals. But working to help them define and realise *their own* expectations is a sure way of maximising the impact of our relationship and the likelihood of their success.

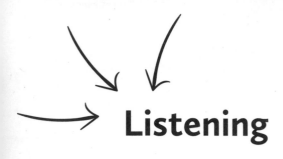

Chapter 5

Listening

A good listener is not only popular everywhere, but after a while he gets to know something.

Wilson Mizner

With the gift of listening comes the gift of healing.

Catherine de Hueck

We've all been there: stood in a crowded room talking to someone when we get a real sense that they'd rather be talking to someone else. Or maybe they'd rather just *be* somewhere else.

Either way, they are not really *present* with us.

For me, one of the overriding feelings I get in this situation is the sense that they're not listening.

Maybe it's the poorly disguised glance at their watch, or the obvious lack of concentration – like saying 'yes' or 'no' to a comment that doesn't really fit with that response. Maybe I catch them looking over my shoulder towards another part of the room.

Awful isn't it?

But why is it so awful? What is it about these kinds of situations that makes them so discomforting when they happen?

The impact of being ignored

Think for a minute about when you've been in a setting like this and someone has stood in front of you but is clearly not really listening. What did it *feel* like? For me, it's things like feeling:

- uninteresting

- worthless

- ignored

- taken for granted.

What do you *think*? I find myself having thoughts like:

- I'm not a very stimulating person to talk to (if I was, they'd be focussed and engaged with me).

- I lack the social value of other people in the room (because they'd obviously rather talk to someone else).

- I'm not respected (because no one who respects me would want to make me feel like this).

- I have something to offer but this person doesn't want it or value it (if they did, they'd at least listen!).

We're all different, but the principle is exactly the same. If someone doesn't listen it impacts on us. It changes the way we feel and the way we think.

Listening as an instrument of change

If the single action of being seen to listen can have this kind of an impact on another person, the implications for those working with children and young people are clear, and huge.

Two things immediately come to mind:

1. Listening has the power to alter the way a person thinks and feels, so I need to respect that and really listen.

2. Helping someone to think and feel a little more positively about themselves is actually quite easy!

Being ignored changes our behaviour

It's not just the way we feel and think that is affected when someone doesn't listen or fails to afford us the respect of concentrating on the interaction. It also affects behaviour.

Think back to being in the room with the person who's not listening to you – they want to leave, they're glancing at their watch or looking over your shoulder at someone else in a different part of the room.

After the initial feelings and thoughts this induces, something else happens. The urge to *act*. To do something that will *change* the dynamic.

Here are some of the things that I might find myself doing:

- Moving slightly to bring myself more into the other person's eye-line.

- Talking more loudly to try to reinforce what I'm saying and ensure that I'm heard.

- Becoming much more animated – gesturing more, moving my feet, being more facially expressive – to grab their attention.

- Using humour and laughter to raise the emotional pitch of the interaction.

- Being provocative, even swearing, to try to snap them out of it and re-engage their attention.

People often do these things, almost without thinking, because they're working to change the situation – to get the person to engage with them. We want them to listen, to hear what we're saying and to focus. So we change the situation in an effort to make this happen.

Sometimes it works and sometimes it doesn't – but the principle is important.

Troubled kids' behaviour is affected too

This principle (that failure to fully listen induces behaviour change) is also true for children and young people.

When children grow up in environments in which their needs are not met, this is almost always one of the problems. No one is listening.

If you've ever watched a video of the 'still face experiment' featuring American developmental psychologist Dr Ed Tronick, you'll know that even the smallest babies undergo stress when their caregivers ignore them.[2]

The experiment was first presented in 1975 but has been replicated many times since. It shows an infant who, after three minutes of interacting with a mother who keeps a 'still face' and remains expressionless, becomes serious and cautious. After making a number of attempts to interact with the mother with no result, the infant withdraws and turns his body and face away from the mother. It provides a clear example of how inattention from the parent is toxic to a child.

So, infants and children who lack parental attention work to get the attention they want. They point, they shout or scream, they change the tone of their voice and they make gestures they wouldn't normally make. They squirm in their seat as the stress of being ignored takes hold.

If this situation persists, if they are continually denied the engagement they need, the reactive behaviour will persist too. Over time this kind of behaviour becomes entrenched. It becomes the norm.

Alongside this, feelings induced by the lack of engagement also continue. Those feelings of worthlessness and being taken

---

2   See https://youtu.be/apzXGEbZht0

for granted become the norm. The child's understanding of themselves – their self-concept – is characterised by feelings of rejection, disconnection and isolation.

Over time, such a child does not learn their own value or how to interact properly with other people.

For many troubled kids this is the root of their problems. Their socialisation is missing a foundation stone – that of being listened to, empathised with, and heard. These children struggle to learn the associated skills of how to relate to other people.

So how do we really listen?

There are a few aspects to this.

Be aware

This is about reminding ourselves, constantly, that we need to listen. It's such a simple thing, but it's very easy to forget. Hearing can be passive. Listening is active. It's something we have to set out to do.

Children and young people can be either the most talkative or the most closed down. And all shades in-between. The chatty ones – often younger – can say so much that we miss the stuff that matters. In the stream of words we lose focus. In this situation it's easy to think that if we get the gist of what they say, that's good enough. But it's not. Hidden in the flood of expression can be vital clues and give-aways that we need to catch.

Conversely, when kids are closed down, quiet or unresponsive it's hard to see beyond what they do say. In our gratitude that they said *something*, we can miss the importance of it. Our relief that the awkward silence is over clouds our clarity of thought about the meaning of what was said.

In both these extremes, and in the more usual degrees in-between, listening is crucial.

Just being aware of the need to listen will help us to tune in.

Be attentive

This takes us one step further on. We've reminded ourselves of the need to focus on the child or young person. Now we need to attend. This is about doing the business of blinkering ourselves to distractions, quietening our mind and listening.

None of us has as much time as we'd like to get everything done. We're all busy. So in order to attend effectively we'll need to do two things: tune out of other stuff and tune into the child.

Even if your diary isn't crammed, I bet your mind is busy with all sorts of disparate and varied thoughts, all vying for your attention. Yep, me too!

We must try to quieten this background noise if our full attention is to be available to focus on the child or young person in front of us.

- Take a minute in the car before you meet them, breathe a little, and think through the purpose of the visit/session/interview/lesson/whatever.

- Take a moment to put yourself in the child's shoes: imagine what kind of day they might have had so far. If you were living in their circumstances, what might you be feeling about meeting you?

- What might their concerns, worries or expectations be about the upcoming encounter with you?

- Are there things from your last meeting that you need to bear in mind today?

Action point: There are practical things you can do. Try making a list of things to do later on, so that you can allow them to slip from your mind without worry. If you've captured them, they don't need to take up any room in your thinking – that can be for later.

The above should give you a general sense of the idea! It's about orientating ourselves to what's about to happen. Getting our mind clear of distractions and our own baggage so that we're free to focus properly on someone else.

Blinkering ourselves in this way is a great method of making the most of what might otherwise be a cursory or even a peremptory encounter.

To listen well, we have to be deliberate.

Feed back now

Now we get to the actual listening itself. This is so much more than just actually opening our ears and attending to the voice of another. It's about the way we communicate this. One of the worst assumptions we can make is that the child or young person *knows* we are listening.

We not only have to listen, but make it *clear* that we're listening.

The person glancing at their watch at the party may *hear* what we say, but they're not really listening. Their body language and demeanour make this abundantly clear – their attention is elsewhere.

Kids from troubled backgrounds – particularly those from homes where a sense of threat and danger were common place – are acutely aware of the physical cues we give. How we look, eye contact, what we do with our hands, proximity, facial expression and movement, all communicate. Our listening can be all the more effective if we employ this knowledge.

Action point: Try using simple nods, the mirroring of facial expressions, quiet mm-ing and the repetition of phrases used while the child is talking to you. These responses can all say, 'I hear you, I'm listening, I get this.'

 Letting the young person know that we're listening is so important. Assuming it and merely opening our ears is a lost opportunity.

Just as we have to be deliberate in focussing our full attention on the child, so we can maximise the benefit by deliberately communicating this using simple in-the-moment feedback.

Remember what has been said

Having listened well and worked at communicating this, we now have to ensure that we don't lose what has been said. Capturing the essence and/or the detail of what's been expressed – in mind or in writing – will be the ultimate proof of whether we really listened or not.

Now, the quality of your memory and the number of children you're dealing with will affect the importance of this for you. Personally, I have to work at this because my memory for spoken details isn't great. Equally, if you have a great memory but you have 30 children to deal with, this can be challenging for you, too!

For some things this will be easy – the very nature of some important conversations means that we'll readily remember them later. Others – perhaps the less obviously important stuff – take a little more effort.

Action point: Try keeping notes for some young people (just using their initials in your mobile phone, as an aide-mémoire, to jog your memory). Looking back at this before you meet them again is one way of getting ready and focussed for the next session. A note like this can also help later, when the more detailed case recording or diary entry needs to be done.

Revisit later

Following contact with a young person, when you next see them, it really helps if you can recall things talked about the last time.

Picking up a conversation, asking after someone or seeking an update on something already discussed is a sure way of helping the child feel listened to. It shows that, not only did we listen well in the moment, but we also remembered it and raised it again on the next occasion.

Whatever your strength of memory or propensity for note-taking, the crucial point is that kids will feel listened to if we refer back to things covered last time. It shows them that we took notice and have had it in mind since – a key message for hildren who may not have had caring adults looking out for them in this way before.

None of us wants to be the person taking a sly look at their watch instead of listening. But by employing these simple principles, we can avoid this and become *active* listeners, thus empowering children and young people to both speak and be fully heard.

Chapter 6

Giving

Goodness is the only investment that never fails.

Henry David Thoreau

It's not how much we give, but how much love we put into giving.

Mother Teresa

We're all happy to give our work time, our advice and our professional guidance to the children and young people we work with. Because that's the deal. Right?

I have a theory that there's a lot more to it than that.

At the start of the book we chewed over the good and bad reasons for working with troubled young people. Now we come to the core of it.

Nuts and bolts

I've seen it a hundred times. Maybe a thousand. Colleagues who grind through the motions of their responsibilities without any real sense of personal investment. No sense of mission. No passion.

It's almost as if they've lost sight of the human element. Forgotten that this is about people. About a child or young person.

My Dad told me about a job he had once. It was in an engineering factory. It was a simple job that involved nuts, bolts and washers.

He'd sit on a stool surrounded by four sacks: one full of nuts, one of bolts, one of washers and an empty one. His job was to take a bolt, put two washers on it and then screw a nut on the end. Then he put the finished item in the empty sack.

That was the job – assembling nuts and bolts. All day long. Bless him!

Now some people treat their work with troubled kids like that. They process them. They run the textbook, work the system, follow the rules…and forget that there's a child involved. And not just any child, but a troubled one.

Here's what that kind of interaction looks like:

- We expect young people to confide in us, to be honest with us, to trust us. This comes at a cost to young people. They have to give us something of who they are – to let us in.

- But we give nothing back. Of course, we supervise, we instruct, we advise, and we smile while we're doing it. But there's not much of *us* in it. No sense of personal giving or investment. It's *one-way traffic*.

This difference between one-way traffic and two-way traffic is often the difference between those who connect with the kids they work with and those who don't.

The monkey isn't enough on its own

You see, you have to *give* a monkeys. We nailed that to the floor in Chapter 1 – that the best reason for working with troubled young people is that we *care*.

The giving that we're discussing here is about making sure that we *communicate* this. Feeling it isn't enough. Believing it isn't enough. We have to get it across to the young person.

We have to *give*.

Remember, these kids aren't used to someone having them at the centre of what they do. They're not used to being the focus of someone who has the power to make their life better. This is foreign territory to them.

That's why they don't respond right away. They may react suspiciously, aggressively or in a noncommittal way. Why wouldn't they?

So, it's up to us to go the extra mile, to dig deep, even when results take time to come.

 It's up to us to keep giving ourselves to the process.

We do this as follows.

Be honest

This is about respect for the young person and fostering their respect for us.

We are dealing with real people, not widgets. We're not processing nuts and bolts or components on a production line. These are children in the throes of development whose learning potential is massive.

We owe it to them as real people to be real ourselves.

So let's break this down into three ways this honest giving of ourselves can happen: speech, feelings and froth.

Speech

If we hide behind professional courtesy and trite replies, we block out the real person; the real us. In doing so we deny the young person the opportunity to hear our authentic voice, which says so much about who we really are.

How often have you listened to a politician on the news and been frustrated when they don't answer the question? Drives you nuts, right? Me too.

Yet we do this to children and young people all the time. We couch our responses in language that we know is opaque. We dance around the handbags instead of dealing with it head on.

Instead, we should honour a straight question with a straight answer.

This week I came across a young person who'd been expecting to move residential placements to one nearer her home. I discovered she'd been told for the last 14 months that she'd be moving 'very soon'.

Fourteen months isn't soon. And it's certainly not *very* soon. This was one very frustrated girl!

No wonder her behaviour was deteriorating. She'd started running away, assaulting staff, refusing to attend meetings – the usual protest behaviours kids exhibit when we lie to them. Because that's what it is when we obscure the truth and serve up flannel instead.

Speaking to the responsible worker, I was told that they were still unaware exactly when the move would take place. But no one had told the child this. Someone needed to be honest with her. Sooner rather than later. It may get a big negative response at the time, but in the long run it'll pay off.

Respect has to have legs, it has to be put into action – truth is one sure way of communicating respect in practice.

Feelings

Here's where we probably fail most often. I certainly do. We shield young people from any sense of our emotional experience. And when it comes to troubled kids, emotions are hot currency because self-regulation is often a key problem to be overcome.

I reckon that parents who fail their children most often do so in this area, too.

Once we get them beyond the picking-up stage – where we rock them back and forth to stop them crying and help them back to calmness again – we don't employ the same effort to helping them control their feelings. It becomes about compliance and we start shushing them and telling them off for expressions of emotion. I speak as a parent who's struggled with this with my own kids.

The kids we work with have often experienced this to extremes – getting attention from adults only when those same adults want them to do something or stop doing something.

And many of them have never experienced that early comforting either. On the journey of helping their kids to learn about feelings, the parents started badly and finished poorly.

Working with such children and young people gives us a chance to make up some of this lost ground. But we can only do so if we let them past the professional facade. They need to see the real person behind the role.

Feelings – in the little things

If we're tired we should say so. If it's been a tough weekend with the kids, why not mention it? Crashed your car or been ill for a few days? Why would you *not* say so?

Now, I'm not saying we should use kids to provide therapy for us in some way. Clearly not.

But somehow to pretend these things are not happening and important to us is to forget that kids can tell how we are. They *know*.

Maybe not the detail. But they *know* when we're not right; when all is not well with us. Acknowledging this is not only more honest, it's more respectful.

Feelings – in the big things (occasionally)

I dealt with a young man once who asked me straight out, 'What have *you* got to teach *me*? What's ever gone wrong in *your* life?' He was angry and he was shouting. I think he just wanted to shut me up! But behind that there was a really good question:

'How can some educated professional who's only here because he gets paid possibly help me?' Powerful stuff!

I told him my wife and I had lost a child to miscarriage a couple of years before. I said it was a really difficult time and that I wondered sometimes how I'd keep going.

I didn't cry. I didn't wait for his advice (obviously). I didn't do it in a way that sought somehow to trump his question or solicit his sympathy. I just answered it simply and honestly. Our relationship moved up a gear after that. Suddenly, I was human. I'd been through some tough stuff, so maybe I *could* help him, after all.

Now this won't happen often. This was a big thing. His feelings were big, and his demand for an answer was strident and unequivocal. But it was also reasonable. So my answer reflected that. But we need to be honest in the little things a lot. And in the big things when it'll serve the child or young person to do so.

> **Action point:** Next time you're talking with a child or young person, ask yourself: will answering this question honestly help this young person in some way? If so, do it.

Froth

This is the stuff that typifies what we're like when we're *not* in work mode. The fun stuff. The unpredictable us. It's the things that make us human, that make us individuals, that set us apart from each other. Kids need to see this sometimes.

I like to make people jump. If I get a chance to hide in a cupboard and jump out on a colleague, a friend or one of my kids, I'll take it. Few things make me laugh more.

So I do this with kids I work with sometimes. Not all the time – that would be weird. Just sometimes.

I remember driving down a very steep hill in the South Wales valleys one day with a young man in the passenger seat. We'd been working together for a couple of years and had a good thing going between us. He was tense this particular morning as we drove to court, because there was a very real chance he'd be sent to custody. Things needed lightening up.

On this particular occasion, as we neared the bridge at the bottom of the hill, I put my hand to my face, braked and screamed as loud as I could. Well he jumped so much he nearly back-flipped into the rear seat!

I was laughing so hard I had to pull over. Then he started laughing. I remember he was trying to swear at me but couldn't manage it because he was laughing so much. Every time we drove down that road after that, we talked about it. (He didn't go to prison that day.)

As you can see, giving ourselves isn't rocket science. It's really just about letting our guard down a little. It's about allowing young people to experience who we really are as *people*, as well as professionals.

Self as an instrument of change

In our efforts to be honest we have to ensure the safety of everyone concerned. That means making sure that the aspects of ourselves that we give away are purely for the good of the young person.

Remember, it's not about *us*!

A guiding principle for helping us stay on the safe side of being honest is to view ourselves and our openness as a means to serve the child or young person. So we should be honest only in as much as it is neutral or will help *them*. It should never be about indiscipline or about meeting *our* needs.

Making the person in the car jump served *him*. He laughed. He relaxed. And, because I knew him well, I knew he'd present better in court in that frame of mind than he would have done if he was still agitated. It served *him*.

Important caveats

- **Speech** – unguarded words can be dangerous. Speaking without thinking is not honesty. It can just be stupid! Words have the power to heal and to wound. So we need to use them wisely. It's possible to *say* how we are, or what we think, without doing damage. We just need to choose our words carefully. Rehearsal is a good safety measure.

- **Feelings** – care is needed here. Off-loading or venting has no place in our interactions with troubled young people. Allowing our emotional state to get the better of us and intrude into conversation is to be avoided. We can give insight into how we are without dumping our negativity on them. Again, if it will serve them, do it; if not, then don't. If in doubt, don't.

- **Froth** – being human and remaining professional is a trick to be mastered! We should work at being relaxed and informal, where our role and the task at hand allows for it. But we can't collude with young people or take sides with them against 'the system'. Snippets of insight into the real life, off-duty, ordinariness of who we are can work wonders. In moderation. We still have our role to fulfil.

So, helping young people to change and progress is less about technique and more to do with the quality and focus of our interactions.

It's my belief that we help more effectively if we share something of the real us.

Chapter 7

Boundaries and Integrity

To know when to be generous and when to be firm – this is wisdom.

Elbert Hubbard

Integrity combined with faithfulness is a powerful force and worthy of great respect.

Gordon Atkinson

I want a dog! I had a dog growing up, as a child, and would really like one now.

Our garden at home is perfect for a dog. It's enclosed on all four sides so there's no risk of escapes. Even the passageway down the side of the house has a gate at the end that is fully dog-proof.

In short, the boundaries of our home mean a dog could have freedom without risk.

Freedom?

Yes, freedom.

We don't normally use the word 'boundaries' in the context of what it *allows* us to do. If you think about it, it's more often to do with what we're *not* allowed to do. Things like the following:

- Walls or fences that mark the edge of and keep people out of our gardens or property.

- Where one country ends and another begins – you can't come in here without a passport and without our permission!

- Jurisdictions – that's your patch and this is ours. You don't have jurisdiction here and we don't have it there.

Whilst each of these could be seen in a more positive light, that's not how it generally works. Boundaries have to do with what we *shouldn't* do, where we shouldn't go, etc.

There's no escaping this. But in the world of helping troubled kids, it might help *us* to see boundaries as something freeing. As something that liberates us. I guess it's a 'half-full' way of looking at things.

Maybe if *we* view it like this, the kids we serve will start to see it that way too.

Professional boundaries

If you've read the previous chapters in this book, you will already be getting the idea that I'm a believer in relational ways of working. That *we* are the main instrument of change for children and young people.

For this to work and for everyone to be kept safe, we need to be aware of how much freedom we have to practise in this way. What are the boundaries that apply to the work we do?

Now we all have different roles with the children we deal with. So it won't be possible to attempt an exhaustive list of dos and don'ts here. But there are some principles that can be applied to most settings that will help us be clear about how to practise well.

The 'good' worker

I recently had a job interview for a promotion. Like all interviews, it was a bit scary!

There were two parts to it: a panel interview with three professionals – senior people with wide experience and influence in the field; and a second panel interview – this time with two young people.

No prizes for guessing which one I was most nervous about. Yep, the kids!

They asked a number of searching questions, including: 'What makes a good worker in the role you are applying for?'

Here's how I answered:

- Know and be good at doing your job (know the role).

- Know and be good with children and young people (know the 'customer').

I think this about sums up the issue of dealing with boundaries and integrity in professional childcare situations.

 It's not enough to be good with young people. We have to know our job, too.

Know your role

Being clear on what our professional responsibilities are is crucial if we are to practise well. It's not good enough to be someone who is personable, friendly, incisive and adept with young people. We have to know our job, too.

This is not just about serving our employers well or doing what we have to do in order to earn our money at the end of the month. It's also about power and advocacy.

Power and advocacy

You see, if we are not completely au fait with our professional function, our remit, the context of our work and what needs to be done, then we can't possibly translate this for children and young people.

Remember, our role is to serve *them*. Not ourselves. Not primarily our employer. But the children and young people who need us and the services we work in.

Someone once said, 'If you really understand something well, you can explain it to a child.' Isn't this all the more true of those who can explain it to a very *troubled* child?

Hiding behind phrases like 'It's complicated' or 'You wouldn't understand' isn't good enough for us or the kids we work with. Their lives have already gone awry and lack power; they need us to be able to simplify and explain what's going on, at a level that fits their needs and understanding.

By doing so we empower them. We give them the insight they need to understand what's happening now and what might happen in the future. In so doing, we free them from some of their fears, their misconceptions and some of the mistrust that is holding them back.

If we know it thoroughly and can explain it clearly, we set kids free from groping around in the dark and just being swept along by the tide of professional systemic momentum.

So, ask yourself the following:

- Can I explain my role to the children I work with?

- In one sentence, what is my job?

- How would I tweet my job description in 280 characters?

This is a real challenge! But it will help us to be ready when we get asked about our role by the children themselves.

Competence

On top of this, of course, the reason we need to *know* our role so well is so that we can *fulfil* it. Explanation alone isn't enough, we have to *do* what's necessary, too. And to do it well.

We all fall into habits of working that limit the effectiveness of what we could be achieving for young people. There may be powers we have that are not being exercised. There may be resources that remain untapped. Opportunities not realised, and so on.

Only when we question ourselves – 'Is there more I could be doing?' – do we stand a chance of avoiding the pitfalls of ignorance and limiting work habits.

Being good at our job means staying open to learning. It means we accept that we don't know it all and that we can *always* improve.

So the first two boundaries that will free us to function well are: *knowing* and being able to explain our role; and *doing* our job competently by constant improvement.

 We must accept that we don't know it all and that we can always improve.

No compromise

As well as ignorance and poor work habits, there are a number of other traps that can hamper or even hamstring our efforts to fulfil our responsibilities well.

Most of these, in some form or another, have to do with compromise. Compromising our role, our integrity, our professional unity or the trust children place in us.

This is what I mean.

Collusion

This has to do with siding with the young person inappropriately. We all want to stand alongside and support them, but we must resist the lure of becoming *like* the child in order to do this.

Children will sometimes say negative things about our colleagues or those working in other agencies. They'll suggest less-than-honest ways of getting what they want. They'll attempt emotional blackmail to tempt us to do certain things.

Avoiding these efforts and retaining a clear sense of integrity is vital. Not only do we risk compromising ourselves professionally, if we yield, but we set a less-than-good example to the children we're trying to help.

Our goal is to equip these children for life. Giving in to collusion won't move them towards this. But, we can acknowledge that where they want to get to *is* valid (expressing frustration, looking for solutions, achieving their goals) and help them find better ways of getting there.

Joining in with negative stuff isn't one of them.

Flirtation

I guess this is about using flattery or some quasi-romantic means to try to move things on or make progress with a service user – most notably, teenagers. Our relational working needs a clear boundary that's well short of this kind of stuff.

There are occasions for all of us where our abilities to communicate, empathise and work with children and young people can tip into over-familiarity. Or maybe adopting a 'bit-too-friendly' way of being. It's not sexual or flirtatious in the usual sense, but we know this is out of line with our role – we've over-stepped a mark and need to rein it back in.

Sometimes children or young people – especially those with precocious sexuality due to abusive experiences – can flirt with us. They begin to behave towards us in ways which would be more akin to romantic or quasi-romantic encounters with peers.

Sometimes transference happens. This is when young people take the feelings they've had towards others in their life, and re-direct them towards us. This can include feelings of a child to their parent, or romantic affection.

Once again, it's our role to spot this and respond to it kindly, but firmly. We must always resist the temptation to 'go with it', because that would be a compromise of safe practice.

Again, equipping children for life means that they learn when this kind of behaviour is appropriate (i.e. within romantic relationships with peers) and when it isn't. Being clear and gently guiding them away from it will also reduce their vulnerability to those adults who might seek to take advantage.

Dilution

This is about those times when a child or young person needs or is asking for information or some response from us, but we don't tell them the whole story. The information is incomplete or worded opaquely to make it easier for us.

One great temptation here is to tell ourselves that we're making it easier and less painful for the *child* by settling for a half-truth or partial response. And this may be true – in the short term at least.

But what happens when they eventually find out the full story? Worse still, when they find out we knew and didn't tell them?

Just like the young woman described in the previous chapter who was expecting to move placement 'soon', but was still there over a year later. It wasn't the truth, it was an easy win for the social worker at the time. But they reaped a bitter reward for it – the girl's behaviour deteriorated, staff were assaulted and she put herself at risk. And all because the truth felt hard to say.

As with collusion and flirtation, dilution is ultimately a betrayal of trust. It's a failure to deal openly, tell the truth and treat children with the respect they deserve.

It also lays us open to the kinds of accusations and allegations we all want to avoid!

Work the process

All of our professional roles have clear responsibilities built in:

- Social workers have child protection procedures.

- Youth justice staff have national standards.

- Foster carers and residential workers have safe-caring practices.

- Custody staff have the regime/routine to guide them.

- Educationalists have their timetable and professional expectations.

- Health staff and therapists have a code of ethics.

- Most of us are subject to some kind of code of practice.

And this is fine – it's as it should be. Getting paid means we have things we have to do to fulfil our roles and responsibilities.

Sailing close to the wind

As any good sailor will tell you, the closer you are to the wind, the faster the boat will go. But it only takes being a little too close and the wind drops out of the sails and you lose momentum. In fact, there's a chance you'll come to a dead stop.

In our practice, we want to sail as close to the wind as we can, using the full extent of our powers, influence and resources to serve kids. But we don't want to cross a line.

In short, unless we do it right, things will go wrong!

Our job is to make sure we dot all the 'i's and cross all the 't's, doing our jobs thoroughly, properly and with integrity.

Resisting the engine

Breaking the rules of sailing by starting up the engine and motoring along isn't really *sailing* at all. There may be times when we're tempted to cross a line to get things done. To speed things up or to get the results we want more easily. But, just like the wind, we can't control everything. We have to work with and with*in* a wider system to achieve results. There's no other way.

So we must do what we have to do, even if it means it takes a while, takes a roundabout route to get there or relies on the timescales of others to get it done. In the end, if we work together, we'll get there!

Compromising, taking shortcuts and leaving something undone or half done isn't an answer. At least not to those who believe in working to the highest standards of professional conduct and personal integrity.

Have your cake and eat it

At no point should our efforts to build relationships with children, to show them respect and establish trust, be allowed to compromise our efforts to do our job properly – to tick the boxes we need to tick. Being a professional means doing things *right*.

At a zoomed-out level, we are agents of society tasked with helping society's troubled children. We have responsibilities in both directions. We owe society the respect of fulfilling the role we are paid to do. We owe the children the respect of building trust and working relationally to further their best interests.

The best of us are those who manage to do both well.

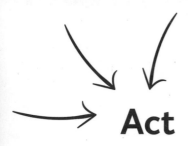

Chapter 8

Act

Speech is conveniently located midway between thought and action, where it often substitutes for both.

John Andrew Holmes

Seeming to do is not doing.

Thomas Edison

I'll never forget a particular meeting which sticks in my memory as one of the defining moments of my career.

The reason was that a young person took over and delivered a withering lecture to the professionals about their incompetence. Here's what happened...

DO something!

David was a savvy, streetwise teenager. His Dad was a drug dealer, his mother was dead and he'd suffered all kinds of abuse and neglect since he was very young. Now, he found himself homeless and in need of somewhere to live urgently.

The problem was that David was a difficult young person to like. And an even more difficult one to look after.

He'd been in and out of foster care and was currently sleeping rough. This emergency meeting was triggered when he was found sleeping in a farmer's barn, where he'd obviously been for quite some time.

Unusually, all the world and his brother had turned up for the meeting – social services, education, voluntary sector agencies, youth justice, housing providers and even a psychiatrist!

The purpose of the meeting was to consider the situation and try to find a solution to David's accommodation problem. Everyone said their piece. And everyone defended their territory:

'That's not our remit.'

'We don't cover that area.'

'He doesn't quite fit our criteria'.

You know how it goes. Everyone wants to say their piece but no one wants to *do* anything.

After all this, David started to speak. Then he summed up his frustration in one cutting conclusion, and I quote:

'You f***ers are really good at talking, but no one is doing anything to help me!'

Actions speak louder

Wow! You could've heard a pin drop.

Not particularly because people were shocked. Not because they were offended or felt the interjection was inappropriate and contrary to the normal social rules – though it clearly was. No one questioned his logic or the accuracy of what he said. So why the stony silence?

Because he was *right*. And everyone knew it.

We'd talked, we'd analysed, we'd considered, we'd asked each other questions and umm-ed and ahh-ed about all of it. But no one was suggesting a way forward.

David had seen this before and he didn't want it to happen again – lots of talking, no real action. No solutions.

Many of you will recognise this as a pretty common occurrence in dealing with complex and difficult situations involving children and young people. But not many get to see professionals brought to book in the way David did it.

 Kids will only trust what we say when we've established a pattern of doing.

Delivery is everything – the 3 Cs

We've talked already about the importance of trust in helping troubled kids. It's central. Without it, true engagement is virtually impossible.

One key way to help young people to trust and engage with us is to *do* what we *say* we'll do. We have to act.

It's back to sequencing again. Kids will only trust what we say when we've established a pattern of doing. It's the only way. There are no shortcuts.

There are a number of implications from all this; we need to:

1. **choose** our words carefully

2. **communicate** clearly

3. **carry through** what we said.

So, here goes…

1. Choosing our words carefully

It's normal to have words trip off the tongue without really thinking about them. We all do it. But it's an easy way of setting ourselves up, and the children we work with, to fail. How? By creating expectations that we can't meet.

For me, I tend to have a series of things I need to get done when I see a young person. This sometimes makes me a poor listener – I'm too busy holding these things in my head, so I don't really focus on what the young person is saying. Or I give a pat answer to something so that we can move on to something else.

This is not good.

The child feels they aren't being listened to and I've 'responded' in a way that confirms it. The truth is that I haven't really responded at all, because I haven't really listened. So my words become meaningless and the child is no further forward – this was David's problem!

If I listen carefully, I can respond carefully.

It's better to be tentative about what we say we're going to do than it is to be certain and promise too much. Over-promising almost always leads to under-delivery – and the cycle of mistrust rumbles on.

Action point: Ask yourself:

1. Is what I'm about to say true?

2. Can the child or young person understand the meaning of what I'm going to say?

3. Am I able to deliver on it?

If you can answer 'yes' to all of these, then you're probably on pretty safe ground when it comes to choosing your words carefully.

---

2. Communicating clearly

This picks up on question 2 in the action point above. Communication is a two-way process. Someone is *communicating* (trying to get a message across) and someone else is being communicated *with* (receiving that message). As the adults in the process, we have to pay attention to both perspectives.

It's so easy to say something or write something to a young person and assume that they understand it. Not that they just understand the *words* we used, but that they understand the *meaning* of the words – and, crucially, that they understand them in the same way we do.

A friend of mine observed a mother at the school gate talking with her young daughter. Here's how the conversation went:

> Child: Mummy, what is sex?
>
> Mother: What do you mean, 'What is sex?'
>
> Child: Well, when I come to ask you for something, sometimes you say, 'Just hang on two secs.'

Imagine what kind of answer the mother might have given if she hadn't checked what the child meant! The child meant 'secs' (as in 'seconds' – the passage of time). The mother might well have heard 'sex' – an entirely different thing altogether!

Check out these two sentences:

> Danger. No swimming allowed.
>
> Danger? No! Swimming allowed.

Both sentences contain the same words, but each has an entirely different meaning. In fact, the *opposite* meaning.

Words can sound familiar and we can think we know what they mean. But do we always understand what *someone else means*, when they use the same words? Clearly not.

 We shouldn't assume that children know what we mean – it's wise to check.

Here are a few things worth bearing in mind (and that I've said myself!) that I'm sure kids don't always understand:

- **Appropriate** is a word professionals use when it's too hard to be accurate. We don't want to say, 'That's not safe', 'You're not old enough to do that', 'That person's care isn't good enough' or 'I don't think you're ready for that just yet'. So instead we say it's not appropriate. This doesn't help the child at all. It's way too woolly and unclear. Better to just explain exactly *why* something isn't appropriate than to use a word that remains meaningless until we explain it fully – in which case we don't need it anyway!

- **Assessment.** This is something most of us have to be involved in sooner or later in our work with troubled kids. It's something that is part of the everyday working world we live in. But it's not always clear to kids what it means. Different professionals and agencies will mean different things when they talk about assessment. Children may well have experienced assessment before – for better or worse – but it may differ from *your* assessment. Don't make assumptions; say what you mean, how long it will take and the kinds of things you'll be looking for. And, above all, what the purpose of it really is.

- **Time.** This cuts in two ways: the assumption that children understand the *passage* of time and can therefore have a sense of how long a period will actually be; and also the use of vague, time-related terms like 'soon'. Many children from troubled backgrounds don't have a sense of how long a week, a fortnight or a month might be. They may also struggle with shorter periods like five minutes, an hour or three hours. This leaves them uncertain and we owe it to them to make sure that we don't use these terms until they do understand. Using a digital clock or an egg timer, and ticking off days on a wall calendar, can be useful ways of helping children deal with the passage of time.

It's not enough merely to take care about the actual words that we use with children. We also have to check their understanding of those words, to be sure that they get *our* meaning, and don't assume an entirely different meaning of their own.

Action point: Ask a child or young person to explain back to you what they think you meant. Then you can be sure they get it, or can add clarification or further explanation if not.

Employing the 3 Cs will ensure that what we say to children will create accurate expectations of what it is that we'll do.

Now comes the doing bit…

3. Carrying through what we said

Words are not enough. Action must follow. We have to actually do the doing. The ultimate test of whether or not we are trustworthy will depend on our ability to follow through, to come up with the goods.

Now this doesn't mean always giving the child or young person what they want. Not at all; none of us can do that. It wouldn't be *right* to do that, in some cases.

But if we're being careful and clear in what we say to children, we must then be mindful that we've created an expectation that we will *do* something. So we need to go on and do it.

It can be really helpful to keep the child informed about our progress in getting something done – a progress report, if you like. This helps them to see that we have them in mind, even when we're not with them, and that we're working on things behind the scenes. All this can help build the child's confidence in us.

Ultimately, though, it's getting things done that shows that we are trust*worthy*.

Do the job

It is easy to sit up and take notice. What's difficult is getting up and taking action.

Honoré de Balzac

This sounds like – and probably is – a statement of the obvious, but we have to actually *do* our job.

Our roles exist because they are felt necessary for the effective help and recovery of troubled children. Someone has decided that our society needs social workers, psychologists, teachers, foster carers, YOT officers, youth workers, therapists, probation staff, police officers, etc. So it's vital that we fulfil our roles well.

Just as we work hard to engage children and build trust with them, so we have to work hard to do a good job. This is why reflective practice is so vital in our field of operation.

I use the following to reflect on my work and test the quality of my own attitudes and actions.

Action point: Ask yourself, 'If this were my child, would I be happy with what I'm doing and the way I'm doing it? Is there anything I could do better?'

Challenging isn't it? But this *is* someone's child. And that child has, in some way, been entrusted to us.

We have a responsibility to do our job. Not just as a series of actions, but as series of actions that are designed to further the welfare of someone who cannot do these things for themselves. They *need* us.

Children lack the power and authority, the confidence and the experience to pull themselves out of the mess they find themselves in. They need adults they can lean on. They need professionals who get what it's like to be a troubled child and are committed to helping.

And committed to helping *excellently*!

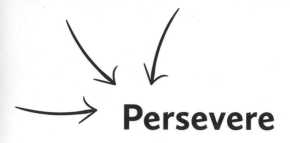

Chapter 9

Persevere

Persistence and determination alone are omnipotent. The slogan 'Press on' has solved and always will solve the problems of the human race.

Calvin Coolidge

*If you've lost your **way**, it's probably because you've forgotten your **why**.*

Anonymous

I remember giving evidence in a child abuse case. The boy had given me a crystal-clear disclosure and the case went to court.

The case was thrown out on a technicality. The perpetrator – the child's father – walked away from court unpunished.

We lost. I was gutted!

Setbacks

Working with troubled children and young people has setbacks – this was exactly that. A big one.

This lad gave me one of the clearest disclosures of sexual abuse I've ever taken. The interview he gave was brilliant. I employed all the training I'd received from the police and others about interviewing victims and child witnesses. I drew on years of experience of working therapeutically with abused children. The evidence was clear.

But circumstances and the law didn't work in our favour in court.

I had to explain the outcomes to the young person. And to his mother – who was now distraught. They both needed a lot of help to understand what had just happened and why justice hadn't been done – at least from their perspective.

Then I went home – I was utterly depressed and exhausted.

The territory

Working with troubled children and young people sets you up for things like this. It comes with the territory. Whether it's:

- a bad day in court

- an assault at work

- a bad shift in residential or secure care

- another placement breakdown

- a young person going missing…again!

- a child who *won't* engage

- a less-than-complimentary inspection

- another agency who won't play ball

- being turned down for funding

- a re-offence, just when you thought you were getting somewhere.

And on it goes.

The three steps forward and two steps back experience is the way it goes with troubled families.

Setbacks and disappointments come to us all, sooner or later.

Keeping going

Most of the children we deal with have experienced all kinds of problems. For many of them their whole development has been delayed or damaged as a result. It's taken time for things to go this badly wrong. And it'll take time – often a long time – for things to be put right.

This is why persistence in our work is so important. There are no quick fixes.

Just as the journey the child has travelled in their life so far has been difficult and fraught with hard stuff, so our professional journey in helping them to recover will be challenging and require perseverance.

They need us to keep going!

Remembering your 'why'

Keeping going is one thing. Keeping going despite constant setbacks and disappointments is another thing altogether – it's really tough.

It takes something pretty powerful to pick us up and dust us down so we can go again. Particularly when it happens time after time.

For me, this takes me back to basics and forces a key question into my mind:

> Why do I do this job and set myself up for these kinds of hassles?

Essentially, I need a reason to get up and carry on after another failure, difficult situation or setback.

It takes me back to my 'why':

- *Why* do I do this job?

- *Why* do I care so much?

- *Why* does the welfare of these children matter so much to me?

- *Why don't* I do something easier and that pays better?

Establishing our 'why' can help us to press on when the going gets tough. It can galvanise our resolve when we're feeling worn down and, maybe, we feel like packing it all in!

Capturing your 'why'

It's worth spending a few minutes thinking about your 'why' and capturing it.

Action point: Do the following three simple things to help you distil your thinking about why you do the job you do with troubled children:

1. Think through what brought you into work this morning. Not the car or a bus! What motivated you?

2. Write a quick list of the reasons you like your job; think particularly about the child-focussed reasons – what they get out of you doing your job. But also what you get out of it.

3. Look over the reasons and motivations, and then cut out as many words as you can. Try to capture the sense of it all in one sentence.

This will leave you with a short statement which, hopefully, summarises your 'why'. If you wanted to, you could then find a phrase or representative sentence that spells out the essence of it. That's what I did.

My 'why'

There, but for the grace of God, go I.

This means a lot to me.

I could wax lyrical for a very long time about why this sentence sums up my motivation to work with troubled young people. But basically, it reflects my view that my life is only as good as it is because I had good parenting and the associated life chances that brings.

Without the love and affection, without discipline and positive role-modelling, without attentive care and patient correction, my life would have turned out very differently.

So differently, in fact, that I might well be in the same predicament as many of the children I've worked with over the years. I'm not a better *person*. I just had better *chances*. Better care.

This is my passion: to work to ensure that every troubled child I encounter has as much of a good *second* chance as I and my colleagues can muster.

I feel emotional as I write this – that's how motivating it is. It is absolutely worth getting out of bed for!

Five benefits of remembering your 'why'

Now, having established and distilled our motivation into a succinct and memorable one-liner, we can remember it and employ it for our own benefit. Here's why...

1. **It keeps you focussed.** Working with troubled families comes with all kinds of distraction, busyness and complication. Dealing with issues and decisions, hard stuff and hard people is easier if we have a clear and present sense of *why* we're doing it in the first place.

2. **It keeps you other-centred.** Our work comes with all sorts of political nonsense – inspections, inter-agency tensions, worker-blaming, etc. But having a clear sense of why we do it helps keep the children we serve central; it helps to keep the work about *them*, not the other rubbish!

3. **It keeps you brave.** Advocacy is key to helping troubled kids. Confrontation, challenge and cage-rattling is part of the deal. Having a sharp sense of why we do it will keep us shouting loudly for those who have no voice of their own.

4. **It keeps you doing the extra.** Anyone who does the bare minimum is not a believer. But those of us who love our work with troubled kids do more. We invest more, we give more, we worry more. Remembering *why* we do it helps us to keep doing the extra.

5. **It keeps you (keeping) going.** Day after day of challenge and hard work is tough. Keeping going is tough. But *keeping keeping going* is another thing altogether. Getting up and starting off again after setbacks – that's when remembering your 'why' really comes into its own.

I think you'll agree, there's real merit in having a clear sense of your own motivation.

 Remembering your 'why' can really help when the going gets tough!

How to remember your 'why'

We know what our 'why' is. And we know the benefits of remembering it. So how do we go about remembering and employing it to help us persist in the work we do?

- **Soul food.** Being a self-starter is hard going, so finding like-minded people can be a massive help. There will be those you work with who see the mission the same way you do. Find these people. Be deliberate in fostering these relationships. We talk about hard things being 'soul-destroying'. So we need to do some active soul-*building*. Well, good company is *good* for the soul. And soul food will help keep you going.

- **Shop talk.** When you've found others of a like mind, use these interactions as a way of feeding your motivation. Talk about why you do the job. Find out what motivates others. This can help you further refine your own thinking and understanding about why *you* do what you do. Having two or three people who beat with the same heart I do for these kids has possibly been the greatest motivator for me when the going gets tough.

- **Memory box.** We make these for children, so why not for ourselves? Find ways of hanging onto the good stuff. Capture the successes at work; keep the 'thank you' cards and encouraging emails. Keep a note of things that go well. Negative stuff is easily remembered. We need to work doubly hard to recall the positives!

- **Objectify it.** A colleague of mine uses a roll of masking tape as a way of remembering her 'why'. It signifies the need for children's voices to be heard (not taped up!). That's what motivates her – she can be a voice, an advocate, for those with no voice of their own. Find something that signifies your 'why', and keep it close – on your desk, in your bag.

- **Be deliberate.** None of this will happen sponta- neously. The press of work, family and friendships will ensure that we are flat out pretty much all the time. So if we are to retain a real and practical sense of mission, we'll have to be deliberate. It won't come to us. We have to make it happen.

So…

Action point: Which of the above things could you do today, that would help you to establish and/or remember your 'why'?

At the end of the day, you and I could probably make a lot more money doing something else. And have a lot less hassle doing it.

So why don't we?

Because we love what we do, and something about doing it gives us a reason to get up in the morning, and to *keep* getting up in the morning.

That's your 'why'.

Distinctiveness

People are quick to judge. And the kids we deal with are easy to judge because they can be difficult and challenging.

Working with these kinds of children and their families means we feel this judgmentalism. We might even feel negatively judged ourselves for *wanting* to do the job.

But these young people need us to stand between them and the finger-waggers – they need that buffer. We have the ability to calm the children and keep them safe, whilst we challenge the society that produced them, but that can also provide the way out they need.

What sets us apart from the crowd is empathy. This is our distinctiveness: we 'get' why these children are like they are. We feel it. We understand that it isn't their fault and that they need help to make it.

This is why we must cultivate persistence. Persistence in empathy. Persistence in the work. In the battle!

 Years of damage can take years of work to undo.

Often the damage can't be *fully* undone, but it can be mediated and diluted, and children can be helped to get past the bad stuff. Their life chances can be enhanced and the likelihood that they won't repeat the same mistakes with their own kids improved.

But this can only happen if we hang in there. If we keep going – even when the going gets really tough.

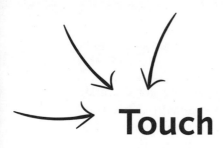

Touch

Touch your customer, and you're half way there.

Estée Lauder

Too often we underestimate the power of a touch, a smile, a kind word, a listening ear, an honest compliment, or the smallest act of caring, all of which have the power to turn a life around.

Leo Buscaglia

Touch? What, touch children and young people?

Yes. Really!

Just think for a moment about the people you came into physical contact with today:

- **Your family** – partner, kids, parents, others in your household. Most of us will have had some kind of physical contact with someone we love today. A pat on the shoulder, a hug, a kiss or holding someone's hand. All these are small, incidental even, but they are important nonetheless and intrinsic to our everyday experience.

- **Colleagues** – those in your workplace, others you encountered throughout the day. Chatting at the photocopier, sitting next to someone in a meeting, handing them some papers or a cup of coffee, or standing around a screen together reading something. Tiny contacts, hardly noticeable – but contacts just the same.

- **Complete strangers** – people you met for the first time, or come across only occasionally. I bet you shook someone's hand today at some point, even though you may not have known them from Adam. So did I.

Touch is normal

Physical contact with other people is part of life. So much so that we don't really think about it.

That's the point here – touching is a normal part of the human condition. It's part of our design. We need it. Troubled kids are no different – they need touch too.

In fact, touch is central to the establishment of healthy secure attachments to caregivers. Imagine trying to parent a child without ever making physical contact. It's a nonsense, not to mention nye on impossible!

As a parent or caring adult, how could we possibly care for an infant without picking them up? How do you deal with a crying toddler if you can't make physical contact with them? You can't – it's nuts even to contemplate it.

Even if we thought we could achieve it, it would be weird – abusive, even – to try.

So, as those committed to working with troubled children and young people, we need to consider how we can incorporate touch into our relationship building, into our work and into our everyday interactions.

Experience of touch

Many young people – particularly those in foster care, residential settings and in custody – have not had the positive experiences of touch like the rest of us.

These kids have missed out on those day-to-day physical interactions through which children learn the appropriateness of touch.

Part of helping them to recover is to give them such experiences – whilst keeping everyone safe.

Children from abusive backgrounds may have some very negative experiences of touch. It may be something they are fearful of, become aggressive about, shrink away from or avoid at all costs. We need to respect this and pace things accordingly.

Negative touch

Some children will initiate situations where touch takes place, but is negative or even damaging.

For example:

- **Assault.** Some young people struggle to control their feelings and will assault others. Part of this for *some* children will be born out of the need for physical contact or about the fearful ambivalence of needing it but hating it too. In many cases this kind of behaviour is subconscious or pre-conscious, but it's there – the need to make physical contact with other people.

- **Restraint.** In residential settings particularly, and in custody, young people will sometimes need to be restrained. After years of working in this field, I'm convinced that, for some, this is about needing to be touched. Or, more accurately, the need to be held. It's about having someone take physical control of them in order to restore some sense of safety and security. To be held is to feel safe. Even if the behaviour that initiates the holding is negative.

- **Harmful sexual behaviour.** Contrary to the popular myth, most such conduct in young people is not about distorted attraction to deviant sexual behaviour. It's about social and romantic incompetence, about acting out abusive behaviour they experienced from adults or about the simple need to feel the warmth and affection of physical touch. For many it's about never having learned where the boundaries lie between normal touch and sexual touch.

I don't think we need to analyse kids' behaviour too much here. But we should acknowledge that for some young people some of their negative touching behaviours flow from the vacuum left by not having experienced appropriate, safe, loving touch at home.

OK touch

I believe it can really help a young person for us to initiate touch, within obvious boundaries, in order to help them experience this positively and safely. For example:

- **Handshakes, high-fives and knuckle touches.** This is my preferred method of making physical contact with the kids I work with. A handshake has a degree of formality about it, so I tend to offer this at first meeting, as well as later on in the relationship. With some young people this will evolve into various hybrid handshakes where thumbs get involved and the hand position changes. I encourage this. Boys go for the handshake more readily than girls, I find; girls seem to prefer the knuckle touch. That said, young people may go for either approach depending on what they feel comfortable with.

- **Back and shoulder pats.** These are usually acceptable to kids once we get to know them a bit more. But I would counsel against rushing – I'd only do this when I felt very familiar and was certain it wouldn't offend. If in doubt, always err on the side of caution. Personally, I'd stick to shoulder pats with girls, rather than back pats; with boys I'd use either. But that's just my preference; you may feel differently.

For this to work it has to feel comfortable and safe, both for us and for the young people. There's no rule of thumb here – except always to exercise caution – but you'll find your own way in it.

Relationship first

If someone I'm not familiar with ventured to touch me without good reason or warning, it'd be a shock.

More than that, it might be offensive, threatening or unpleasant (or all three!). So clearly this out-of-the-blue approach isn't acceptable and should be avoided – always. If we dive in without warning, we should be ready for an equally and opposite physical reaction – again, without warning.

Children and young people are no different from us; touch naturally occurs in the context of relationship. Trust comes first; other kinds of familiarity – including touch – come later on. Sometimes *much* later on.

 Use caution. We earn the right to touch – we must never assume it.

Asking permission

I have a rule of thumb about touch that has served me well so far: if I have even an inkling of doubt about a young person's ease with it, I avoid the touch. Or, if I think it has merit and is appropriate, I ask permission first. For example:

- **If a young person is upset.** I might say something like: 'I can see you're upset, I feel for you, do you mind if I put my hand on your shoulder?' Or, if I was more confident they were OK with the touch: 'I'm just going to put my hand on your shoulder, is that OK?' Then I would move to touch slowly and watch their posture and body language to check any reticence. As always, if in doubt, don't touch.

- **Safe touch first.** Sometimes I might venture a safe touch first and see the response. For example, in the same situation described above, I might cup someone's elbow with my hand and ask if there's anything I can do to help. Both the touch and the words communicate concern without being overly pushy or familiar. And if the child is unhappy they can easily disengage the touch and move away without it feeling like a big deal.

Physical contact can be a great calming influence. Its use can speed up a child's return to emotional equilibrium. Used unwisely it can have the opposite effect too!

Employing these kinds of checks and balances should keep us and the young people safe. It should also allow us to deploy the positive impact of touch to the advantage of those we work with.

Touching and calming

When infants cry, we pick them up. Yes, we rock them, we talk to them, we check out what's wrong and we put it right. But, before all of this, we pick them up.

This parent–infant touch is central to the establishment of attachment relationships and all the myriad developmental benefits of attuned care.

Just as parents pick up their babies in order to care for and calm them, we too can employ touch as a simple but profound way of helping troubled children and teenagers back to calmness when something unsettles or upsets them.

We do it with adults too.

If someone close to us suffers a bereavement, we'd probably give them a hug. Why do we do that?

- **Because we can't fix it** – there's nothing we can do to bring the person back. 'Fixing' the problem is not an option. But we need to *do* something, to let the person know we understand and that we care.

- **Because it communicates** – and so much more than words or mere gestures ever can. In this sense actions really do speak so much louder than words. And it only takes a second.

Our friend doesn't need us to fix the problem. They know that we can't. But a simple touch says that we 'get it', that we care and that we're alongside them in the tough stuff.

If it works with adults, then why not with troubled kids when they're unsettled or upset?

Benefits of touch

We've established that touch is an essential and valuable facet of normal human development. The absence of it is therefore *abnormal.*

So, in helping troubled children and young people to recover from their problem pasts, we must try to include touch in our repertoire of caring practices.

Just as *we* may not appreciate the benefits of touch until it is absent, so the benefits of touch to young people may not be explicit, to them or to us.

So what are they?

- **Equality.** Our work with troubled children means we have a degree of power over them. Not just because we are adults. But because we are professionals who have responsibilities and the authority to carry them out. The way we discharge our roles means we can affect young people's lives.

 Touch communicates a degree of equality. It says, 'You're a person too.' There is something humanising about being touched.

- **Value.** We tend not to make physical contact with people and things we distrust, dislike, don't understand or are fearful of. We touch whom and what we value, what's close to us; because what's important and what we trust won't hurt us. In this way we can say clearly – without words – that we value someone and are prepared to communicate that through physical contact.

- **Affection.** Here we stray into sensitive territory. Affectionate touches like kissing and caressing obviously have no place in professional childcare settings. But touch can still communicate appropriate affection. Not only does it say, 'I trust you and I value you.' It can also say, 'I feel for you and I care about you.' In this way touch communicates affection, liking. Often it's the *combination* of appropriate touch and kind words that together communicate care and affection. It takes us beyond the merely professional and into the human, interpersonal domain.

- **Respect.** When someone feels equal, valued and cared for, they are necessarily respected. This may take some time to sink in and show benefits in terms of increased confidence that impacts behaviour. But there is a direction of travel in this process that leads there eventually. Touch of the kind we've described and within the boundaries outlined is an essential part of this journey for troubled kids. They won't get there without it.

Touching young people appropriately, safely and in the context of trust and relationship is powerful.

It can enhance and augment our other efforts to aid recovery for children who desperately need it. If we are committed to working developmentally, we must consider incorporating safe touch.

A quick summary

- If your agency has specific policies around this, stick to those. But…

- I find that a simple shake of the hand is a good way to connect with boys. And a handshake or a knuckle touch with girls.

- It's a small thing and not everybody's preference – that's OK. Do what you feel comfortable with, with what feels *authentic* to you.

- Remember, relationship and trust are the pre-requisites. If in doubt, don't touch!

- But I find it really helpful in building a bridge and humanising the interaction. That little shot of dopamine and oxytocin helps too!

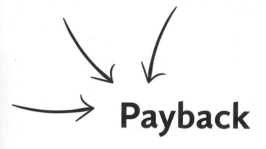

Chapter 11

Payback

The only reward for love is the experience of loving.

John le Carré

There is no greater joy nor greater reward than to make a fundamental difference in someone's life.

Sister Mary Rose McGeady

I love my work. Really love it. In fact, I'd struggle to think up something better that I could be doing with my life.

But I don't do it for nothing. I don't do it just for the love of it, either.

I do it for the buzz – it's a worthwhile thing to do. And I do it for the dosh – I have bills to pay and an unhealthy appetite for chocolate, real ale, pasties and prosecco! You might be a hummus and lentils person, but the principle's the same. We have to earn a living and we want to feel good doing it.

So let's look at the rewards of working with troubled kids.

Seeing children change

Most of my friends and family have a vague sense of what I do for a living. But most of them don't know the detail or anything approaching it. Why would they?

But most people I venture to tell about it say something like 'Oh, I could never do that' or 'That must be really tough.'

Well, *they* probably couldn't do it (any more than I could do their job) and it *is* tough, but there are some real joys in it too.

I often respond to people's balking at the idea of my work by saying, 'Yes, it is tough, but when you see children starting to change and flourish, there's nothing quite like it.'

And this is even more the case when we know something of the suffering and damage they've endured before they came to us. The more serious and life-threatening the illness, the more joy and celebration at the cure. Isn't that true in our work too?

I've wept at times when I've read what has happened to a child. But then I've wept again when I think about how they've pulled through and moved out into the sunshine of a recovered life.

 Yes, it's challenging. But the rewards are legion!

Delay the reaper

I have the names of eight children written on the front page of my diary. I added another one just this week. All eight of the kids named there are now dead. I worked with them all.

The raw reality of life for many of the children in the nation's care system and allied services is that they may not live very long. Without intervention many would not reach maturity.

But in the busyness of life and work, it's all too easy to forget this. To miss the very real prospect that the child or young person in front of us at work today may not make it if things don't change.

But things *can* change.

I remember a young man I worked with in a substance misuse project. We were talking about his life and the problems he faced with long-term depression and thoughts of suicide.

He looked at me with real gratitude and said, 'Sometimes I wake up with the overwhelming urge to kill myself. But I walk up here instead and talk to someone. Things seem better then.'

Wow, that's a win, if ever there was one!

Think back to the children and young people you've dealt with. How many of them might not be here today, were it not for your intervention and the work of colleagues from other agencies – the help they received from caring adults?

As one of the quotes at the start of the chapter says, *that's* making a difference in someone's life!

Celebrating prevention (the invisible investment)

The trouble with our kind of work is that we don't often get to see the positive results first hand.

One of the reasons for this – if not the main one – is that most of the time we are working to *prevent* harm. Or to undo the problems caused by previous harm.

Yes, we can have a sense that we did some good, that we helped someone move forward a little or prevented some kind of further harm.

But we rarely get the chance to celebrate a life transformed. Mainly because that may take a lifetime to achieve, and most of us move on or lose touch with those we've worked with, way before that happens.

Either way, it's a long old job. And we probably won't be there, years later, when the child or young person realises what they've been saved *from*. If they ever realise at all.

So, somehow, we have to find a way of reminding ourselves that what we do makes a difference. Because of our work, bad things don't happen.

We need to keep in mind the things we *prevent* and satisfy ourselves with knowing that things are better because of what we did.

What didn't happen

Whilst we can rarely know for sure what exactly we prevented, it's not too big a leap to identify some general things that might have happened had we, and our colleagues, not done our jobs. Here's what I mean:

- **Greater harm.** Those involved in child protection work on the premise that it's better to do something to avert what might happen. That's an invisible investment. An investment in stopping something. It's hard to celebrate what didn't happen. But we really should!

- **Further offending.** The youth justice system is set up to prevent and reduce offending. Preventing it in those who are susceptible; reducing it in those already doing it. Both are worthy goals. But they are impossible to measure, because when they succeed, nothing happens – offending doesn't happen.

- **A life in custody.** Some young people spend time in a secure children's home or secure training centre; they might have offended or be there for their own welfare. When they get the help they need and find some stability and purpose for their lives, they don't tend to enter custody again. A lifetime spent in the revolving doors coming in and out of prison is prevented.

- **Suspicion and isolation.** In most settings it's the *people* who form the greater part of the intervention. It's less about what we do and more about the people doing it. Through being valued and cared for, kids learn to trust and value themselves. They are saved from a life of loneliness and social isolation. It *doesn't* happen.

- **Ill health.** We know that troubled children are at much greater risk of future physical and mental health problems. These are reduced or even alleviated when we intervene. But, thankfully, we never see the reality of how their lives *might* have been. Because it *doesn't* happen.

- **Trans-generational problems.** When we offer therapy and interventions to help children deal with the damage they've suffered, we prevent them repeating it all in their own families. At the very least we reduce potential future damage. But we don't see them when they become parents. We don't get to count the children of the children we worked with, and pat ourselves on the back for preventing harm to the second generation. Or the third. We don't see what might have happened had we *not* intervened. More on this later.

In all these cases, the joy is in what *doesn't* happen. The kids themselves may never fully realise what might have been.

But we know. And that's part of our reward!

 We need to keep in mind the kinds of things we prevent.

Progress

One of the ways we can enjoy the rewards of our labour is to celebrate small gains. If we always wait around for the big wins, we can wait years before the next one comes along. But, for those with eyes to see them, there are lots of things to celebrate here and now.

One teenager I worked with really struggled to engage with me. We spent weeks just doing that initial trust building that in most cases would be over in a few sessions. But he was having none of it.

He shifted in his seat. He constantly got to his feet and walked over to the door to look through the glass panel at what or who was in the corridor outside. He fidgeted incessantly and spoke with a stream of consciousness that made conversation almost impossible.

So I went with it. I listened. I was patient and calm when he walked away, changed the subject or when he ended the session early by voting with his feet.

After about three months of this, things changed. Not much. But they changed. He started to make some eye contact. Again, it wasn't much, but it was there. He stood up less, walked around less, changed the subject less and, occasionally, listened to what I said, instead of speaking over me constantly.

Small gains, but gains nonetheless!

It was noticing and holding on to these small bits of progress that helped me to keep going for the big ones. Eighteen months later we were in a completely different place in our work together. But change came slowly.

Learning to notice and celebrate the small wins along the way means we get some reward *now*, rather than hoping for something bigger later.

> **Action point:** Think about a tough case you're working on right now. Spend a few minutes reflecting on where things were when you first started and what has changed for the better. Write it down somewhere.

Trans-generational impact

As a colleague of mine is fond of saying, 'All of these kids we work with will have sex and most of them will have children of their own.'

Our work not only gives us the opportunity and the delight of helping *this* child to recover, to grow and to change. We also have the privilege of affecting the way they will parent their own children in the future.

Empathy is not a skill you can teach someone using a worksheet or a series of lessons. That would teach them *about* empathy. To learn to be empathic, someone has to have been empathised *with*. This is the privilege we have – we get to help troubled children and young people learn a skill that will help them. It'll help them not only to be better people, but to be better parents.

So, rather than reacting to their children's cries, perhaps with irritability or annoyance, they might respond with a little more patience, meet the child's needs and nurture them back to calmness again. In this snapshot alone lies the power to transform someone's parenting.

What an amazing thought: that the way we deal with and respect the children in our care might impact the next generation and help to break the cycle of inter-generational problems that so many families face.

What an incredible prospect and reward for us, that we might be the key to unlocking the fortunes of a family that's had three or four generations of kids coming into care. They may not have been born yet, but their future life chances have been enhanced because of what we did today.

Let's read that again:

 The children of the kids we work with may not have been born yet, but their future life chances have been enhanced because of what we did today.

Wow! That's the reality, and the reward, of what our efforts can achieve!

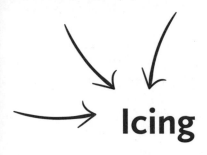

Chapter 12

Icing

Sometimes when we are generous in small, barely detectable ways it can change someone's life forever.

Margaret Cho

There are some things that transport our work with young people into a different league. Things that mark us out from the crowd. Things that can really promote our connection and relationship to another stage altogether.

This is what I'm calling the icing on the cake. It's the stuff that exceeds our set roles, our professional obligations.

In this chapter I want to examine a few of these things.

Remembering

I recently met up with a former colleague of mine from some years back whom I hadn't seen for a year or more. He'd rung for a catch up, but also to ask my advice on something very specific. A couple of days before we met, I remembered it was his birthday coming up. Not just any birthday, but his 50th.

After we'd been out for a bite to eat and a chat about what was on his mind, we made our way back to the car park to go our separate ways again. Just before leaving, I dug a bag out of the boot of my car – his birthday present. He was speechless; clearly moved by the gesture.

Now why was this?

I'm sure that remembering was a key part of it – he hadn't opened the gift, so it can't have been the quality or otherwise of what I bought him. It must have been that I *remembered*. At some point over the preceding few days I'd had him in mind. He didn't know it until this moment. But he liked it. We all do!

This same scenario can play itself out in small ways during our work with troubled children and young people.

- **Names** are important early on in the working relationship. Remembering not just the name of the young person themselves, but the names of family members, other relatives, even the dog! It communicates that we've made the effort. Also, names are important. They are intrinsic to who we are; they identify us. Having to ask someone their name for a second or third time is not only a bit uncomfortable, it can hold up our efforts to build trust.

Action point: Make notes of names (yes, including the dog!). It sounds obvious; but my poor memory has got me into trouble more than once. The habit of writing names down has been a huge win, such that I now have a reputation for remembering people's names!

- **Birthdays** are very important, especially for kids in the care system or in custody. In these circumstances what should be a joyful, fun time can be a real nightmare. A time when all the things missing in their lives are brought to the fore. Remembering and making the effort to personally mark children's birthdays has obvious benefits. Doing so as a professional can never replace or somehow dilute the sting of a child's loss of family. But it can say loudly and clearly, 'Someone values you. Someone remembered you. Me!'

Action point: Put young people's birthdays in your diary along with a reminder a week or so beforehand. This will buy you time to get them something, even if it's just a card. I always have a stock of cards around so I can deliver on this even when I've not had the time or forethought to plan in advance.

- **Losses.** These children have often suffered more loss than many adults four times their age. Multiple changes of parental partner, constant house moves, school changes, family rejections and losses of sibling relationships. As well as some complex and sometimes horrifying bereavements of close family members or friends. The anniversaries of key losses can be difficult times. Knowing about and remembering these can be key to helping children to cope, come to terms with and appropriately mark such key events.

Action point: Has a child you're currently working with suffered a key bereavement? If you can, find out the date, the person's name and what happened. Can you bring this up with the child sensitively and help them mark it in some way?

It's so easy to underestimate the import of these things. They may seem to be outside of our usual brief, or 'not really our job'. But they can play a key role in helping us build trust and engagement with children and young people who need to feel safe and held by someone who knows them, holds them in mind and is trustworthy.

That person could be you.

Effort

This is about going above and beyond. It's about 'going the extra mile'. Is there something you could do that would communicate to this child that you've had them in mind and made an effort to do something for them?

I spoke to a colleague once who explained how she'd bought a gift for a teenage girl she was working with.

The girl was distraught about the adoption of her three-year-old sister. The girl's social worker had been working with her to try to help her come to terms with the situation and process some of her sense of loss. The gift she bought was a small double picture frame where a photo of both girls could be kept.

This was a master stroke! Here's why:

- **Sensitivity.** What she did spoke of her awareness of the child's current challenges, her state of mind and the needs these might give rise to. What she did flowed out from this sensitivity.

- **Specificity.** The gift was very specific to the child and her situation. It was targeted, if you like. It met a very specific need in a way that was equally specific.

- **Super-duper** (sorry, struggling for alliteration there!). It was above and beyond what she *had* to do. It went beyond the expectations of the child and the obligations of the professional role.

It wasn't an extraordinary gift. It wasn't an expensive one either. But it was well-thought-through and spoke volumes about noticing, remembering, thoughtfulness and sensitivity.

It took effort. And it worked. The degree of engagement, trust and respect for this small gesture helped accelerate the progress this young person made. Not just because it addressed a specific need that she had – to mark and remember the loss of a sister – but because someone thought of her and made the effort to do something to help.

Action point: Is there something you've thought of doing to encourage or help a child you're working with, but haven't yet got around to doing? Is there a young person you think needs a boost at the moment? Take a few minutes to really think through what might help them. Then crack on and see the difference it can make!

Honouring

The power of encouragement is greatly under-estimated.

I had an email this week about some training I took part in last week. The person just wrote me a quick message to say how much she'd enjoyed the training and how some of the stuff we talked about had helped her in her work this week. She mentioned a young person she was helping and attributed some very recent progress to the training.

I was over the moon!

What had taken my colleague less than five minutes to write had completely transformed my day. I then passed the message on to another colleague who had helped me with the training, and she was encouraged too. Happy days!

For us, this kind of thing happens relatively often. Relative, that is, to the amount of encouragement the children we work with get. Most of us will receive encouragement of one kind or another fairly regularly – even if it's from those who love us and are therefore biased.

Nevertheless, it has a really positive impact. It builds us up. It lifts our spirits and puts a spring in our step. And why not? After all, someone took the time to tell us that what we did was worthwhile.

Action point: Be on the lookout for successes and positives in the lives of the kids you work with. Even the slightest win is worth celebrating.

Humour

> *A sense of humour is part of the art of leadership, of getting along with people, of getting things done.*
>
> Dwight D. Eisenhower

Getting along with people – some very difficult ones, sometimes – and getting things done is our bread and butter. So humour can be a great help along the way.

Now we are all different and we have a different sense of what is funny and what isn't. But we can all use humour as a tool to help troubled children and young people.

Here's what the appropriate use of playfulness and laughter can achieve:

- **Perspective.** Good comedians take everyday situations and see the funny side of it. They re-enact things we all do and point out the humour. We can help children to develop a different perspective on things by doing the same. Not in mockery or insensitively, obviously, but by showing them that it's possible to look on life differently – it doesn't all have to be seriousness and problems.

- **Safety.** We laugh most when we feel safest. Think back to when you last laughed so hard you nearly cried. I bet you were with someone you felt completely safe with – close friends or family members, probably. Troubled children can be helped to feel safer when we laugh together. It humanises us and levels the playing field a little – this promotes safety.

- **Memories.** When we laugh, we remember. Sharing a joke can create a situation that readily comes back to mind later on. How often have you thought back to something funny that happened, and then laughed all over again? Exactly! So have I. Troubled kids need this too. Many of their memories are laden with pain and regret, questions and deep emotional hurt.

So why not overlay some of this with the sensitive use of humour about things in the here and now that they can look back on later with a wry smile?

- **Intersubjectivity.** This happens when two people's subjective states interact; when two minds share the same time, space and emotional experience, if you like. Laughter is great for this. It's emotional, but it's positive. We can be a different sex, have different ages or have many other *objective* differences, but share the same moment, *subjectively*. This helps build attachment and trust. Troubled children, particularly those with poor parental attachment, need this. Humour can help provide such experiences.

- **Relationship.** Essentially, humour can be a great way of promoting and maintaining relationship. It's about communication, responding to each other and sharing thoughts and laughter, and it's about being *people* – not client and professional – together.

You might be thinking, 'But I'm not a very funny person.' Neither am I. But we each have things that amuse us. If nothing else, we can learn to laugh at our*selves* and use a little self-deprecation to make fun.

Much of what we do is serious. Some of it is *very* serious. So being deliberately playful and/or humorous can introduce an element of joy into the work that lifts both us and the child to a new and positive place.

Action point: How can you introduce humour and fun into the way you work? Find out what makes a child laugh and use that to help them. How could you employ a degree of self-deprecation to help a child to feel more like your equal and to trust you that bit more easily?

Not a cake

You could argue that many of these things are not necessary. After all, a cake is still a cake, even without the icing, right?

Well, yes it is. But wouldn't we all really rather have both? It's not a *proper* cake without icing!

So it is with our jobs. We can do the basics, tick off the things on our list and fulfil our obligations. But we wouldn't be entirely happy if that's all we did.

So let's work at doing the extra. Let's really think about how we can give these kids the taste of something sweet!

Chapter 13

Your No.1 Client

People who care for others tend to be neglectful of one thing. Themselves.

Jonny Matthew, Looking After No.1: Self-Care for People Working With Troubled Children

Think about it – when was the last time you took time out, made a thorough assessment and planned an intervention…for yourself?

I bet it was a while. Have you ever done it?

In my experience of 30-plus years working professionally with children and young people, there is one thing that keeps coming back to mind:

 People who care for others tend not to care for themselves.

It's as if the altruism and empathy that drives us stops at our front door. It rarely gets inside and impacts on the way we view and treat ourselves.

The danger is that the negative impact of the difficult work we do *will* eventually get inside, if we don't take steps to avoid it.

Fit for purpose

We're on a mission. The work we do is more of a calling than a job. A vocation. If you took time out to establish your 'why', you will have a clear sense of what motivates you to take on the challenges, rather than do something more straightforward that pays better and is a lot less hassle.

Because it's a mission, our roles take a lot out of us. It's more than just meetings, keeping records, discussing cases with colleagues and dealing with funding issues. All of these domains are laden with the *kind* of work we do. It's *qualitatively* demanding. And, at times, it can feel overwhelming.

To work well, then, we have to be fit. OK, it helps to be physically fit, of course. But I'm talking about being attentive to our general well-being.

Action point: Ask yourself, 'How well am I?' Yes, think about your sleep pattern, your diet and your physical health. But also about your stress levels, your relationships, and how confident you feel. Rate yourself out of 10.

Compassion fatigue

One of the things I am acutely aware of in my work is that I spend a lot of time in other people's heads!

I am constantly making assessments of what others need: how they're doing, what progress they're making (or not!), what's coming up for them, how my input is being perceived and the timing of the next step. It can seem never ending.

Whatever your role, you will have daily challenges that may not seem great, individually, but can accumulate into a burdensome weight to carry. Over time, this can lead to compassion fatigue.

A close friend of mine once said to me about the daily drip-drip effect of working with difficult stuff: 'Why does everything have to matter so much?'

This sums up our problem. If we were working in a factory making widgets, the only thing that would matter is whether or not we've done our job well enough to produce widgets. That's it.

For us it's different because most of what we do *really* matters. A lot!

 We are in the business of changing lives.

Impacts

Below are some of the things we can expect to come calling when we care for others for a living.

General stuff:

- disturbed sleep (struggling to sleep, waking a lot, nightmares, etc.)

- lower confidence

- decreased pleasure in things we normally like doing

- agitation and anxiety

- reduced motivation

- losing track of our thoughts (forgetting, poor recollection, etc.)

- struggling to focus (distractedness, reduced concentration span, etc.)

- lack of productivity

- heightened irritability

- feelings of hopelessness.

Physical stuff:

- stomach complaints (irritability, nausea, etc.)

- headaches

- stiff neck and shoulders

- tiredness/exhaustion

- poor appetite.

There are lots more, but you get the idea. Now we all experience some of these things from time to time. But when we don't give proper attention to self-care, we set ourselves up for a long list of potential issues that we could well do without.

Regardless of the personal impact, if we are trying to cope with all this on top of doing an already very demanding job, we are setting ourselves up to fail. And we are also never going to be able to properly help those children and families we are trying to serve.

We have to help ourselves if we are going to successfully keep helping others.

Nose to the wall

A neighbour once asked me to put his chickens away in the evening. He was away from home overnight and was concerned the neighbourhood fox would come calling!

So, after tea, I ventured through my garden to the connecting gate which gave access to his garden. As I approached the gate I tripped on something and fell headlong, hitting my forehead on the concrete gate post. It almost knocked me out.

Walls are great things. But if you hit one hard, the wall always comes off better. (Don't try this at home!)

After a few years of working with troubled kids, particularly in the sexual abuse field, I hit a wall of a different kind. A metaphorical wall of stress.

The impact of the work got the better of me; it sneaked up behind and ambushed me:

- I was physically shattered but struggling to sleep.

- I went completely off my food.

- My hobbies felt like chores, so I stopped doing them.

- My energy levels were almost at zero.

- My neck and shoulders felt like concrete and ached incessantly.

- The very thought of work made me want to creep back under the duvet.

- My mind was endlessly awash with thoughts and worries about kids at work.

- I felt sick. Most of the time.

A quick comparison of this list with the ones in the previous section is all it takes to see that I'd burned out.

Despite thinking that I could handle pretty much anything, despite my qualifications and experience, regardless of my usual self-confidence and gung-ho approach to life, I was almost dead on my legs. No energy. No motivation. Nothing left to give.

Something had to change.

 To keep helping others, we must first help ourselves.

Making the change

Sometimes it takes a crisis to galvanise us to action. It certainly did with me.

Once I'd come to terms with the fact that I wasn't invincible and didn't have the resilience I thought I had, I needed to do something about it. I needed to make some changes.

Here's what I did:

- **Got some clinical supervision.** This took a while to organise, but it paid off massively and is still something I benefit from. Now all the staff in the team have it available to them regularly. If your agency doesn't or won't provide it, think about paying for a session privately. Even if it's only every now and then, you'll reap the benefits. If you think you're not the kind of person who needs this, then you almost certainly are and need to act on it quickly!

- **Started taking lunch breaks.** Everyone says they don't have time for lunch. I know what that means; I've said it a myriad times myself. But it's nonsense. All we have to do is get up, leave the desk (or wherever your work places you) and take a break. Go for a walk, sit somewhere else and eat something. That's all it is. Keep the time free in your diary and stick to it. Five minutes is better than nothing. Half an hour could change your whole day!

- **Diarised non-face time.** I started managing my diary so that I had one day a week where I didn't see children face-to-face. I was working in therapeutic work at the time and needed some regular time out during the week where I wasn't exposed to the traumas and challenges of abused children. I used Wednesdays for doing case recording, going to meetings, report-writing and other non-direct work. This is about managing the *kind* of work you do to get the balance right.

- **Spread out my leave.** This is about spacing annual leave more evenly across the year. I took less leave each time, but took leave more often. So instead of having a good break at Christmas and then waiting for nearly six months or more before another holiday, I would put in other breaks inbetween times. Shorten your main breaks slightly so that you can take more long weekends. If you are due time off in lieu, then take it! Put it in the diary and make it happen. Little and often is much healthier as it makes for a better overall pace of work across the year.

These were just some of the things that I did to address the fact that the work got the better of me. You may have other things that will suit your work setting better.

The key is to be realistic and keep it practical. Good intentions won't help – real changes will.

> **Action point:** Could you begin doing any of the things in the list above? Look over it again and think about which one would be the easiest for you to implement. Then give it a go!

Practical hacks

Here are a few other things that you could consider doing to help you avoid burnout and keep yourself fit for purpose:

- **'I can't do it all.'** Telling yourself this is a great place to start. It'll get done eventually, but not just yet. Not today. Doing what you *can* do is as good as it gets. The rest isn't your problem. Write this little phrase down somewhere – a sticky note on your desk, in the front of your diary, on your screen-saver. Reminding yourself of this regularly might just help you lift your foot off the throttle a little and make for a more even pace.

- **Sort stuff.** When tasks start to mount up we can buy ourselves some time and focus by prioritising them. Sort things out into urgent, important and neither urgent nor important – then prioritise the tasks. This will help you do the important stuff first, but it will also feed positively into your efforts to remember that you can't do it all.

- **Make a list.** Please don't feel patronised; you may well do this already, but it's a good habit. It helps to 'capture' what needs doing and lessen the sense of panic! On your list, only include things that fall into the 'urgent' category. Leave the rest for now. Ignore it deliberately. It'll be important...*eventually*. But leave it for now. There are lots of great mobile phone and browser apps that make this easy.

- **Work the list.** Having made the list of urgent stuff, now crack on and work your way through the list. If you manage to tick off all the urgent things, you can continue on and make progress on the important stuff, too! If, like me, you tend to add things to your list that you've already done, this all makes for a nice glowing sense of achievement. And why not!

- **Dominate email.** Email is a real pain in the proverbial. It has a tendency to dominate our thinking, pinging away while we try to get other things done, and generally making a nuisance of itself. Having set times in the day when you check your email will help stop it being a distraction. It'll stop you getting drawn into other things. And *other people's* things. At some point, you will really benefit taking the time to look at and adopt one of the 'inbox zero' methods of email management – it's massively helped me be more efficient as well as taking away that awful pressure I feel when my inbox is full.

- **Diarise everything.** Putting non-appointments in your diary can be liberating. It helps us be realistic about what we can get done in a day. It can also be great for helping us to say 'no' (more on this in a minute). So try to diarise things like time to do paperwork, time to plan for a meeting, time for email and time to think through a case.

 If it's in the diary, it tends to get done.

- **Say 'no' to stuff.** Diarising non-appointments also means you can say 'no' to other things that people ask you to do. Because you know and can say that you have that time allocated already. While writing this chapter I had a request to read and comment on something 'by next Tuesday'. Because my diary is now full, I *know* I can't do it. So I said exactly that. I didn't need to make up some waffly excuse, because I know *why* I can't do it. Saying 'no' is difficult and takes some courage, but it's *very* liberating! I dare you to try it.

- **Raise it in supervision.** If the pace never slows, make sure you raise this in supervision. Ask for it to be noted that things aren't getting done and that your efforts to be more efficient aren't helping either. Discuss solutions. Consider other options. Be creative. But don't sign the supervision notes if you're not happy. Because we deal in people's lives, we have a heavy sense of responsibility to carry. But we can't be the whole agency, only our part. If our part is unmanageable, the agency needs to acknowledge this and take up the load.

- **Consider the nuclear option.** If we can't carry the kids, we certainly can't carry the organisation. Neither should we try. If your agency is placing an unrealistic and unachievable workload on you, then it's time to reconsider. If nothing changes, despite doing all of the above, maybe it's time to move on? Even just thinking about this can help lessen the burden a little! Part of good self-care is ensuring that you are working safely. It isn't safe if you feel you're unable to do your job properly.

I'm sure that many of these things aren't new – maybe none of them are. Like me, you've probably heard and tried many of them before. But that's fine. Better to be trying to take better care of yourself than to plough on and hit the wall.

Action point: Which of the above things could you do today? Is there one that you could adopt and do without too much effort? Give it a go. Baby steps are better than no steps at all.

Act now

The impact of our work can be subtle at first. Then it accumulates slowly. And, if we don't address it, it eventually gets the better of us.

Burnout is a stealthy enemy!

One of the biggest challenges with avoiding burnout is the feeling that 'I'm doing OK'. But we can't afford to keep going just because we think everything is going well. We have to stay diligent and be proactively self-aware of the possible impact issues of our work. We also have to do something about it.

Action point: Start by answering these quick questions:

1. How does my work impact on my well-being? (Be honest!)

2. What changes, big or small, do I need to make to look after myself better?

3. Which simple change can I make today to begin this process?

Go for it!

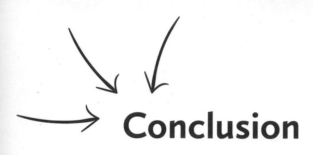

Conclusion

There can be no keener revelation of a society's soul than the way it treats its children.

Nelson Mandela

How do you finish a book like this, when already a host of other things come to mind that would help us to be better helpers of children in need?

If you've read this far, it's probably because you are committed to just that – being better.

You certainly won't be a finger-wagger or you would have given up and thrown this book across the room ages ago!

Maybe the thing that separates us out as dedicated childcare professionals – of whatever hue – is that we are acutely aware of two things:

1. how much we have to learn

2. how much our work matters.

Learning

I have often used the analogy of holding something with an open hand, as a way to describe how we might approach our professional roles.

We can either grip it tight, be defensive, assume we know it all (even passively) and jump through the hoops our roles set out for us.

Or we can hold it out with an open hand – as if to say, 'I don't have all the answers', 'I'm doing my best while I look for even better ways' and 'Looking back, I could have done that differently, and I will if I'm in that situation again'.

That makes you a learner. And, in my view, it makes you a better helper – and someone who will be continually improving throughout your working life.

If my kids were ever in need of professional help, I'd like them to encounter people like that. So why shouldn't someone else's kids find that in us?

> **Action point:** In the Introduction, I encouraged you to wreck this book! Now, why not go back over the notes, underlines, crossings out and highlights you made while reading? Look back over the action points. Which ones will you take forward, which ones will you remember and which ones will you allow to change your practice?

This is how we learn.

The soul of the work

The Nelson Mandela quote at the beginning of this chapter is one of my favourites. It says something profound and challenging to our society about the importance of how we treat our children. In his view, that reflects the *soul* of any society.

But what is the soul of our work?

We are not dealing with children, per se, but with our society's most troubled and challenging children. They are a subset of the whole, a minority; but they are perhaps the most important litmus test of how well we are doing, as a culture.

For me, the soul of this work is about principles:

- It's about not judging children for the problems brought on by others.

- It's about speaking up for those who can't speak up for themselves.

- It's about employing the privileges of relative wealth, education and power to promote the interests of children who have none of these.

- It's about challenging social policy and service provision to serve the real needs of troubled children rather than the felt or unfelt obligations of those with no real needs at all.

And perhaps most of all...

- It's about a belief in the power of relationship to change a child or young person's life for the better.

I believe that if we constantly strive to practise in a way that reflects the principles laid out in this book – and others I've missed – we will be doing a fine job of working to promote these noble principles in the lives of the children we serve.

Recommended Reading

The following books give us an insight into the child's perspective. A short review of most of the books can be found on my website (JonnyMatthew.com).

Canfield, Jack and Hansen, Mark Victor (2013) *Chicken Soup for the Soul: Teens Talk Tough Times*. Edited by Amy Newmark. Cos Cob, CT: Chicken Soup for the Soul.

de Thierry, Betsy (2016) *The Simple Guide to Child Trauma: What It Is and How to Help*. London: Jessica Kingsley Publishers.

de Waal, Kit (2017) *My Name is Leon*. London: Penguin.

Hughes, Daniel (2009) *Attachment-Focused Parenting*. New York: W.W. Norton.

Jensen, Frances E. with Nutt, Amy E. (2016) *The Teenage Brain: A Neuroscientist's Survival Guide to Raising Adolescents and Young Adults*. New York: Harper.

Leve, Ariel (2016) *An Abbreviated Life*. New York: Harper.

Siegel, Daniel (2002) *The Developing Mind: How Relationships and the Brain Interact to Shape Who We Are*. New York: Guilford Press.

Webb, Robert (2017) *How Not to Be a Boy*. Edinburgh: Canongate Books.

Index